John F. Longres, PhD
Editor

Men of Color:
A Context for Service
to Homosexually Active Men

*Pre-publication
REVIEWS,
COMMENTARIES,
EVALUATIONS . . .*

"**T**his book may well become a classic on the identity struggles faced by gay men of color. . . . offers rich insights into the cultural beliefs that help explain homosexual conduct and gender identity in men of color. . . . must reading for professionals and lay readers who want to understand men of color who have sex with men."

Herman Curiel, PhD
*Associate Professor
University of Oklahoma
School of Social Work*

Harrington Park Press

Men of Color:
A Context for Service
to Homosexually Active Men

Men of Color:
A Context for Service to Homosexually Active Men

John F. Longres, PhD
Editor

Men of Color: A Context for Service to Homosexually Active Men, edited by John F. Longres, was simultaneously issued by The Haworth Press, Inc., under the same title, as a special issue of *Journal of Gay & Lesbian Social Services,* Volume 5, Numbers 2/3 1996, James J. Kelly, Editor.

Harrington Park Press
An Imprint of
The Haworth Press, Inc.
New York • London

ISBN 1-56023-083-5

Published by

Harrington Park Press, 10 Alice Street, Binghamton, NY 13904-1580 USA

Harrington Park Press is an imprint of The Haworth Press, Inc., 10 Alice Street, Binghamton, NY 13904-1580 USA.

Men of Color: A Context for Service to Homosexually Active Men has also been published as *Journal of Gay & Lesbian Social Services*, Volume 5, Numbers 2/3 1996.

The development, preparation, and publication of this work has been undertaken with great care. However, the publisher, employees, editors, and agents of The Haworth Press and all imprints of The Haworth Press, Inc., including The Haworth Medical Press and Pharmaceutical Products Press, are not responsible for any errors contained herein or for consequences that may ensue from use of materials or information contained in this work. Opinions expressed by the author(s) are not necessarily those of The Haworth Press, Inc.

Library of Congress Cataloging-in-Publication Data

Men of color: a context for service to homosexually active men / John F. Longres, editor.
     p. cm.
    Includes bibliographical references and index.
    ISBN 1-56024-803-3 (THP : alk. paper). -- ISBN 1-56023-083-5 (HPP: alk. paper)
    1. Social work with gays–United States. 2. Social work with minorities–United States. 3. Gay men–Services for–United States. I. Longres, John F.
HV1449.M46 1996
362.8–dc20
                                             96-35141
                                              CIP

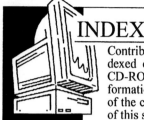

INDEXING & ABSTRACTING

Contributions to this publication are selectively indexed or abstracted in print, electronic, online, or CD-ROM version(s) of the reference tools and information services listed below. This list is current as of the copyright date of this publication. See the end of this section for additional notes.

- *AIDS Newsletter c/o CAB International/CAB ACCESS . . . available in print, diskettes updated weekly, and on INTERNET. Providing full bibliographic listings, author affiliation, augmented keyword searching,* CAB International, P.O. Box 100,Wallingford Oxon OX10 8DE, United Kingdom

- *Cambridge Scientific Abstracts, Risk Abstracts,* Environmental Routenet (accessed via INTERNET), 7200 Wisconsin Avenue #601, Bethesda, MD 20814

- *caredata CD: the social and community care database,* National Institute for Social Work, 5 Tavistock Place, London WC1H 9SS, England

- *CNPIEC Reference Guide: Chinese National Directory of Foreign Periodicals,* P.O. Box 88, Beijing, People's Republic of China

- *Digest of Neurology and Psychiatry,* The Institute of Living, 400 Washington Street, Hartford, CT 06106

- *ERIC Clearinghouse on Urban Education (ERIC/CUE),* Teachers College, Columbia University, Box 40, New York, NY 10027

- *Family Life Educator "Abstracts Section,"* ETR Associates, P.O. Box 1830, Santa Cruz, CA 95061-1830

- *Family Studies Database (online and CD/ROM),* Peters Technology Transfer, 306 East Baltimore Pike, 2nd Floor, Media, PA 19063

(continued)

- *HOMODOK/"Relevant" Bibliographic Database,* Documentation Centre for Gay & Lesbian Studies, University of Amsterdam (selective printed abstracts in "Homologie" and bibliographic computer databases covering cultural, historical, social and political aspects of gay & lesbian topics), % HOMODOK-ILGA Archive, O. Z. Achterburgwal 185, NL-1012 DK, Amsterdam, The Netherlands

- *IBZ International Bibliography of Periodical Literature,* Zeller Verlag GmbH & Co., P.O.B. 1949, d-49009 Osnabruck, Germany

- *Index to Periodical Articles Related to Law,* University of Texas, 727 East 26th Street, Austin, TX 78705

- *INTERNET ACCESS (& additional networks) Bulletin Board for Libraries ("BUBL"), coverage of information resources on INTERNET, JANET, and other networks.*
  - JANET X.29: UK.AC.BATH.BUBL or 00006012101300
  - TELNET: BUBL.BATH.AC.UK or 138.38.32.45 login 'bubl'
  - Gopher: BUBL.BATH.AC.UK (138.32.32.45). Port 7070
  - World Wide Web: http: / / www.bubl.bath.ac.uk./BUBL/ home.html
  - NISSWAIS: telnetniss.ac. uk (for the NISS gateway)
  The Andersonian Library, Curran Building, 101 St. James Road, Glasgow G4 ONS, Scotland

- *Mental Health Abstracts (online through DIALOG),* IFI/Plenum Data Company, 3202 Kirkwood Highway, Wilmington, DE 19808

- *Referativnyi Zhurnal (Abstracts Journal of the Institute of Scientific Information of the Republic of Russia),* The Institute of Scientific Information, Baltijskaja ul., 14, Moscow A-219, Republic of Russia

- *Social Work Abstracts,* National Association of Social Workers, 750 First Street NW, 8th Floor, Washington, DC 20002

- *Sociological Abstracts (SA),* Sociological Abstracts, Inc., P.O. Box 22206, San Diego, CA 92192-0206

- *Studies on Women Abstracts,* Carfax Publishing Company, P.O. Box 25, Abingdon, Oxfordshire OX14 3UE, United Kingdom

- *Violence and Abuse Abstracts: A Review of Current Literature on Interpersonal Violence (VAA),* Sage Publications, Inc., 2455 Teller Road, Newbury Park, CA 91320

(continued)

SPECIAL BIBLIOGRAPHIC NOTES

*related to special journal issues (separates)
and indexing/abstracting*

- ☐ indexing/abstracting services in this list will also cover material in any "separate" that is co-published simultaneously with Haworth's special thematic journal issue or DocuSerial. Indexing/abstracting usually covers material at the article/chapter level.

- ☐ monographic co-editions are intended for either non-subscribers or libraries which intend to purchase a second copy for their circulating collections.

- ☐ monographic co-editions are reported to all jobbers/wholesalers/approval plans. The source journal is listed as the "series" to assist the prevention of duplicate purchasing in the same manner utilized for books-in-series.

- ☐ to facilitate user/access services all indexing/abstracting services are encouraged to utilize the co-indexing entry note indicated at the bottom of the first page of each article/chapter/contribution.

- ☐ this is intended to assist a library user of any reference tool (whether print, electronic, online, or CD-ROM) to locate the monographic version if the library has purchased this version but not a subscription to the source journal.

- ☐ individual articles/chapters in any Haworth publication are also available through the Haworth Document Delivery Services (HDDS).

CONTENTS

ABOUT THE EDITOR

John F. Longres, PhD, is Professor of Social Work at the University of Washington. He was born to Puerto Rican and Cuban parents and raised in the South Bronx.

Dr. Longres is active in the National Association of Social Workers and in the Council on Social Work Education where he has been Chair of the Commission on Minority Concerns, Chair of the Commission on Publications and Media, and a member of the Commission on Gay and Lesbian Concerns. He presently is Editor of the *Journal of Social Work Education.*

He has a long list of publications in major social work and sociology journals. He is the author of *Human Behavior and the Social Environment* which is in its second edition and which is published by Peacock Publishers, Inc. His primary area of research is race and ethnic relations and he is presently involved in a study comparing anxiety and mood among a national probability sample of African-, Latino-, and non-black, non-Hispanic children and adolescents.

Foreword

Over twenty years ago, the American Psychiatric Association changed its position about homosexuality. It stopped including homosexuality as a psychopathology and, except for ego-dystonic homosexuality, removed the term from its influential Diagnostic and Statistical Manual. Shortly thereafter, the Board of Directors of the National Association of Social Workers (NASW) agonized about whether to permit its Delegate Assembly to vote on a supportive policy statement. Regrettably, the social work profession did not easily accept the de-pathologizing of sexual orientation. The NASW Board compromised; they did permit a resolution regarding homosexuality but did not permit the formation of a guiding policy statement.

While the social work profession was initially hesitant to promote a progressive stance in regard to civil rights and the provision of appropriate services, the profession has moved gradually to respond to the many concerns of the community, including the HIV/ AIDS pandemic. The National Association of Social Workers now has a number of supportive policy statements regarding gays and lesbians and those who are HIV/AIDS infected. In addition, the Council on Social Work Education has revised its Curriculum Policy Statement, the guiding framework for accredited baccalaureate and master's degree programs, and now mandates the inclusion of sexual orientation in these curricula.

It is not enough to promote affirmative policies and mandate the incorporation of curriculum content if the available human services literature is limited. The creation of literature on gay and lesbian issues has been much more extensive in areas other than the social

[Haworth co-indexing entry note]: "Foreword." Garcia, Alejandro. Co-published simultaneously in *Journal of Gay & Lesbian Social Services* (The Haworth Press, Inc.) Vol. 5, No. 2/3, 1996, pp. xv-xvii; and: *Men of Color: A Context for Service to Homosexually Active Men* (ed: John F. Longres) The Haworth Press, Inc., 1996, pp. xiii-xv; and: *Men of Color: A Context for Service to Homosexually Active Men* (ed: John F. Longres) Harrington Park Press, an imprint of The Haworth Press, Inc., 1996, pp. xiii-xv. Single or multiple copies of this article are available from The Haworth Document Delivery Service [1-800-342-9678, 9:00 a.m. - 5:00 p.m. (EST). E-mail address: getinfo@haworth.com].

services. For that reason, it is important to note that the *Journal of Gay & Lesbian Social Services* is a welcome addition to the literature. Now, John F. Longres has provided additional leadership in the development of a special edition on social services for gay men of color.

Our society asks much of a gay man of color. He must be able to communicate in the majority white society, in his own cultural group, and among fellow homosexuals. These respective groups make great demands of him to be loyal to them, with appropriate punishments for any deviance from what they consider to be cultural norms. He faces racism, homophobia, and a demand for ethnically-congruous behavior. The life experiences of gay men of color, who are sexual as well as racial minorities, put them in double jeopardy. The pressure to maintain two identities that is brought on by the racism of the majority community and the homophobia of his ethnic community results in a unique form of marginalization. As a gay person of color he must constantly face the question of his primary identification: does he primarily identify as gay or as a person of color? Gay men of color are often forced to choose between one identity or the other and in so doing may have to forsake an essential part of themselves. If gay men of color are to deal effectively with their marginalization, both their ethnic community and the gay community will need to better understand their situation.

As many articles in this volume note, the term "gay men of color" may not be broad enough to include the full spectrum of sexual orientations found among men of color. Many authors have struggled to come up with other terms, but these other terms–"men who love other men," "men who have sexual relations with other men," "homosexually active men"–are also unable to capture the range of behaviors and attitudes found among men of color. Yet the articles in this volume do explore the issues and provide new insights into men who are often ignored in the human service literature.

The HIV/AIDS pandemic has added urgency to learning how to help the infected and their families as well as to preventing further infection in communities that are bearing the brunt of this terrible disease. Although the articles in this volume deliberately do not focus on HIV/AIDS, they do provide needed information about sexual attitudes and practices which is useful in fighting the disease. In some ethnic communities, the role a man takes in a homosexual encounter determines whether he is perceived (or perceives himself) as homosexual or heterosexual. Since ethnic minority communities often understand the term "homosexual" differently than the white community, erroneous information about risk factors leaves many men and women of color vulnerable to this disease.

Similarly, many believe that ethnic and racial minority groups are more homophobic than European Americans. Yet these articles challenge this idea and provide deeper insights into how male homosexuality is incorporated in other cultures.

Xenophobia, homophobia, and fear of HIV/AIDS combine to make the United States a difficult society for gay men of color. This volume is an important contribution to the literature and should encourage a better understanding of the complex lives of gay men of color–*bakla*, *berdache*, two-spirit men, *de ambiente*, and others– among social service providers from any group. Through this encouragement, we may begin to develop human services that are sensitive and responsive to their sexuality and their ethnicity.

Alejandro Garcia, PhD
Professor of Social Work
School of Social Work
Syracuse University
Sims Hall 302
Syracuse, NY 13224-1230
agarcia@social.syr.edu

Preface

In putting together these original articles I had a number of aims in mind. Paramount, of course, was that I wanted to give special attention to men of African, Asian, Latin American and Native American descent. The burgeoning literature on homosexual conduct and identity, while not overlooking diversity, does not exactly put it center stage either. Although there is a vast anthropological and historical literature that provides insights about homosexuality in other societies, there is comparatively little on men from minority and immigrant groups in the United States.

I also wanted articles about men of color that did not focus exclusively on AIDS. This was the case even though I realize that AIDS is the most devastating catastrophe that homosexually active men must face, that men of color are hit harder by this catastrophe, and that these articles are likely to be read by educators, trainers, and social service personnel who are working in HIV prevention and support. I wanted instead articles that provided a context for working with homosexually active men of color regardless of the specifics of their service needs. In spite of the personal and political horrors of the AIDS epidemic, we need to keep in mind that our chief purpose is to foster gay affirming social services. Not long ago, social service professionals treated homosexuality as pathology and deviance. In many sectors of American society–including services provided through ethnic and racial communities–this continues to be the case. My chief aim therefore was to add an ethnic dimension to the literature on homosexual conduct and identity and thereby improve services for men from all communities.

[Haworth co-indexing entry note]: "Preface." Longres, John F. Co-published simultaneously in *Journal of Gay & Lesbian Social Services* (The Haworth Press, Inc.) Vol. 5, No. 2/3, 1996, pp. xix-xxiii; and: *Men of Color: A Context for Service to Homosexually Active Men* (ed: John F. Longres) The Haworth Press, Inc., 1996, pp. xvii-xxi; and: *Men of Color: A Context for Service to Homosexually Active Men* (ed: John F. Longres) Harrington Park Press, an imprint of The Haworth Press, Inc., 1996, pp. xvii-xxi. Single or multiple copies of this article are available from The Haworth Document Delivery Service [1-800-342-9678, 9:00 a.m. - 5:00 p.m. (EST). E-mail address: getinfo@haworth.com].

The articles in this volume are to be appreciated for their unique contributions to the literature. Rosemary Ryan, Roger A. Roffman and I compare identity, networks, and social support patterns among European-, African- and Latino-American men who sought services from the Aries Project, an HIV prevention program. Larry D. Icard lays out an ecological assessment model that can be used by social service professionals working with African American men. Terry Tafoya and Douglas A. Wirth provide an historically based description of Native American men that ends with their own special vision for clinical services. Carlos E. Zamora-Hernández and Davis G. Patterson thoughtfully review the literature on Latin American men and Felix I. Rodriguez does the same with regard to Filipino men; both end with insightful implications for social service providers. Sue Sohng and Larry D. Icard provide an historical examination of Korean norms and attitudes on homosexuality and follow it with an interview with a Korean immigrant that includes recommendations for service providers. Finally, Larry D. Icard, James Williams and I discuss an applied research agenda for gay men of color that derives from the need to improve the delivery of social services.

Although the articles are to be appreciated on their own terms, I am intrigued by three underlying themes that hold them together for me. The first is the idea that homosexuality is indeed a social construction of reality. The second is that the American (and European) gay rights movement has had a profound impact on all groups. Third, although the pull of the gay community is strong, the pull to retain ethnic identities is equally strong.

Almost all the articles show that homosexuality varies culturally and historically. In European American society, having sex with someone of the same sex regardless of what one may do in the sex act, constitutes sufficient behavior for a gay or bisexual identity. In Native American, Filipino, Latino, and African American societies this does not appear to be the case. Sexual behavior rather than sexual object determines homosexual identity in these societies.

Tafoya and Wirth document the many words (i.e., *nadleeh, bote, winkte*) that Native American peoples use to describe cross-dressed men who took on special roles within society and who generally assumed the "feminine" role in sexual relations with "normal" men. Rodriguez indicates that the word *bakla* is used by Tagalog-speaking Filipinos to describe "a man who acts like a woman." He points out that the men who have sex with bakla consider themselves, and are seen by others, as heterosexual. Zamora-Hernández and Patterson point out that the separation between sexual object and sexual behavior is also fundamental to understanding Latino men. They write that homosexual identity refers "almost exclusively to the person assuming the receptive-passive role." They add that the "active" person does not usually think of himself as homosexual; for him, contact with a homosexual may even boost his sense of masculinity.

Homosexuality also varies historically within cultures. Christian missionaries and American mores altered Native American cultures and the "two-spirited" men of today do not function within Native tribes as they did in the past. Rodriguez suggests that changes in the meaning of homosexuality in the Philippines can be traced from pre-colonial, to colonial, and post-colonial times. Zamora-Hernández and Patterson describe the changing attitudes about homosexual conduct and identity in Latin American countries today. Icard shows how historical changes are reflected in the behavior of individuals; he confirms that the meaning of homosexuality is different in adolescent, adult and older adult African Americans today. The major implication for practice in noting these cultural and historical differences is that immigrant and minority communities may have a very different idea of who is homosexual than the majority, including the white gay community.

In spite of different constructions of homosexuality, the articles make clear that the gay rights movement, embodying the principal that gays and lesbians should be assured equal rights, is having a profound impact on all groups. The gay rights movement, with its more inclusive definition of gayness, is seen explicitly or implicitly as a desirable movement. Sohng and Icard learn, from their interview with a Korean man, that a desire to participate in an open, gay community can be an important reason for immigration. Icard suggests that homophobic community norms act as a spur for African American men to explore life in the white gay community. Although Latin American countries and the Philippines give a certain amount of legitimacy to homosexuality, men who do not want to be stuck in limiting, culturally proscribed roles or who would like more freedom in their lives are attracted to the gay rights struggle taking place in the United States. Along these lines, Rodriguez points out that in addition to the traditional bakla and his straight partner, westernized gay couples can now be seen in Manila. Even Native American "two-spirited" men have organized on behalf of change in their own communities and more visibility in the gay white community and in American society more generally.

From this perspective, it is not surprising that although Ryan, Longres and Roffman believed they would find evidence for a different kind of homosexual among their African- and Latino-American clients, they in fact found very little difference between them and their European-American counterparts. Although homosexually active men who do not consider themselves homosexual may eschew even those programs that reach out for them, it is clear that many men of color are finding friends and lovers within the white, gay community.

While men of color are attracted to the white gay community and to the possibility of a more open lifestyle, they are not ready to reject their own ethnic communities. In part the reason is that the gay white community has its own fill of racism and ethnocentrism and men of color don't easily find a comfortable niche within it. Although Ryan, Longres and Roffman find that Latino- and African-American respondents show a great deal of involvement in the white community, they also find that white gays do not show a similar involvement with men of color. The Korean immigrant interviewed by Sohng and Icard also reports that while he is attracted to gay white men, these same white men don't appear to be attracted to him. Rodriguez also calls attention to the "painful and constant ambiguity" endured by Filipinos as a result of racism in the United States.

But more importantly, men of color do not reject their communities because, in spite of any homophobia in them, they still offer a fundamental source of identity and strength. Zamora-Hernández and Patterson write of the deep affection for family among Latin men; family ties are comforting in spite of their inhibition of a collective gay identity and community. The mixed feelings of the Korean immigrant are poignantly captured in the interview by Sohng and Icard; their young man appears in a crisis, drawn and repelled at the same time by both his native and his adopted cultures.

Homosexually active men of color are often caught in a dilemma. They must choose between their ethnic and sexual identities; They must either put ethnicity before gayness or gayness before ethnicity. Icard captures the dilemma well when he acknowledges that until recently African-American men were forced to "find their anchor in either the white gay community or the heterosexual African American community." It may be predicted, however, that the lure of sexual freedom, coupled with the comfort of old traditions, will lead to a new synthesis. Icard notes that a "black gay community" is emerging; It first appeared during the Harlem Renaissance but it is being revitalized today. It promises to be a subculture of both the gay and African American communities. Similarly, Tafoya and Wirth suggest that a gay subculture is also emerging within the Native American community. Since the 1980s, they report, a Native American "Lesbigay" organization has been forging a strong sense of support among Native people and their friends. Any of us who have lived in large cities are familiar with bars and organizations that are segregated along racial and ethnic lines. In the 1993 march on Washington many men marched as ethnic contingencies. Out of these, the gay-hyphenated communities of the future are likely to emerge.

John F. Longres, PhD
Professor of Social Work
University of Washington
Seattle, WA 98195
longres@.u.washington.edu

Acknowledgments

To Jim
who brought all the pieces together

The articles all turn out to come out of Seattle or the University of Washington. This was not my intent. When I started this project I myself was not associated with Seattle, nor were several of the authors whose works are represented here. Although two were already in Seattle, it just sort of happened that six of us ended up here, coming more or less at the same time and independently of each other. I say this not to apologize for the regionalism that may be reflected in the articles but to actually celebrate the intellectual life that I have found through the University of Washington.

I want to give thanks to James J. Kelly and Raymond M. Berger for giving me the opportunity to do this special volume. Not only did they give me an excuse to turn my professional attention to an important issue but they provided me an opportunity to meet and come to deeply respect a whole new set of colleagues. My work with the authors represented in this volume was not only pleasant but stimulating and exciting. My greatest pleasure in doing this volume was getting to know and make friends with the authors. My respect and appreciation to Larry Icard, Davis Patterson, Felix Rodriguez, Roger Roffman, Rosemary Ryan, Sue Sohng, Terry Tafoya, Douglas Wirth, and Carlos Zamora-Hernández.

[Haworth co-indexing entry note]: "Acknowledgments." Co-published simultaneously in *Journal of Gay & Lesbian Social Services* (The Haworth Press, Inc.) Vol. 5, No. 2/3, 1996, p. xxv; and: *Men of Color: A Context for Service to Homosexually Active Men* (ed: John F. Longres) The Haworth Press, Inc., 1996, p. xxiii; and: *Men of Color: A Context for Service to Homosexually Active Men* (ed: John F. Longres) Harrington Park Press, an imprint of The Haworth Press, Inc., 1996, p. xxiii. Single or multiple copies of this article are available from The Haworth Document Delivery Service [1-800-342-9678, 9:00 a.m. - 5:00 p.m. (EST). E-mail address: getinfo@haworth.com].

xxiii

Sexual Identity, Social Support and Social Networks Among African-, Latino-, and European-American Men in an HIV Prevention Program

Rosemary Ryan
John F. Longres
Roger A. Roffman

SUMMARY. On the assumption that effective practice requires knowledge of cultural differences, this study examines the responses of over 400 African-, Latino-, and European-American men seeking services to reduce the risk of HIV infection. The responses of the men to questions about sexual identity, social support, and social networks were compared. Relatively few statistically significant differences were found. Possible confounding conditions as well as the implications for practice and research are discussed. *[Article copies available from The Haworth Document Delivery Service: 1-800-342-9678. E-mail address: getinfo@haworth.com]*

Rosemary Ryan, PhD, is Research Assistant Professor, Innovative Programs Research Group, School of Social Work, University of Washington, 4101 15th Avenue NE, Seattle, WA 98195. John F. Longres, PhD, is Professor of Social Work, School of Social Work, University of Washington, 4101 15th Avenue NE, Seattle, WA 98195. Roger A. Roffman, DSW, is Associate Professor and Director, Innovative Programs Research Group, University of Washington, School of Social Work, Seattle, WA 98195.

[Haworth co-indexing entry note]: "Sexual Identity, Social Support and Social Networks Among African-, Latino-, and European-American Men in an HIV Prevention Program." Ryan, Rosemary, John F. Longres, and Roger A. Roffman. Co-published simultaneously in *Journal of Gay & Lesbian Social Services* (The Haworth Press, Inc.) Vol. 5, No. 2/3, 1996, pp. 1-24; and: *Men of Color: A Context for Service to Homosexually Active Men* (ed: John F. Longres) The Haworth Press, Inc., 1996, pp. 1-24; and: *Men of Color: A Context for Service to Homosexually Active Men* (ed: John F. Longres) Harrington Park Press, an imprint of The Haworth Press, Inc., 1996, pp. 1-24. Single or multiple copies of this article are available from The Haworth Document Delivery Service [1-800-342-9678, 9:00 a.m. - 5:00 p.m. (EST). E-mail address: getinfo@haworth.com].

1

INTRODUCTION

An important issue in the delivery of health and social services is the degree to which variations exist in the beliefs, motivations, and behaviors of clients from different ethnic and racial groups. According to the cultural model of ethnic sensitive practice (Green, 1982; Longres, 1991), individuals from these groups vary culturally in experiences, expectations and behaviors and as a result are likely to seek, accept, and use help differently. If we are to deliver effective services, it is of paramount importance to be responsive to the cultural content that clients bring to interactions with service providers.

Ethnic sensitivity is at least as much an issue in delivering services to sexual minorities as it is in serving heterosexual clients. In this paper, we use data collected from clients of an HIV prevention program to examine similarities and differences among African-, Latino- and European-American men who have sex with men. In addition to comparing demographic characteristics, we also compare the groups with respect to sexual identity, social support, and social networks. Despite sampling limitations, the data can shed light on differences and similarities between men of color and those of European descent. The data can also shed light on the degree to which ethnicity moderates the hostility that men who engage in same gender sex face in their everyday lives.

Finding acceptance and support can be especially difficult for gay and bisexual men of color, who confront not only prejudice against homosexual conduct within their ethnic communities (Beame, 1982; Ernst et al., 1991; Icard et al., 1992; Singer et al., 1990; Stewart, 1991), but also racism in the predominantly European-American gay community (DeMarco, 1983; Loiacano, 1989; Marín, 1989; Stewart, 1991).

A number of authors have observed that homosexually active ethnic minority persons are hard pressed to find acceptance that is uncompromised by racism, homophobia, or both. For those who have the option, a solution is to form or join organizations for sexual minorities of color. Those without this option are often forced to choose between their ethnic or sexual identity or to split their allegiance between two communities, both of which offer only

partial acceptance (Beame, 1982; Icard, 1986; Johnson, 1982; Loiacano, 1989).

Several studies have demonstrated that sexual behavior and identity are not synonymous. Some people have sex with others of their
own gender without ever assuming a gay or bisexual identity (Doll
et al., 1992; Klein et al., 1985; Lever et al., 1992). This separation
between behavior and identity has been noted in particular among
African- and Latino-American men (Doll, et al., 1992; Magaña &
Carrier, 1991; Marín, 1989; Singer et al., 1990; Stewart, 1991).
Insulation from gay community norms that enhance HIV risk reduction behaviors and underestimation of risk because they do not
identify as gay are thought to contribute significantly to higher rates
of homosexually transmitted HIV infection among African- and
Latino-American men (Doll et al., 1992; Marín, 1989; Peterson &
Marín, 1988; Singer et al., 1990; Stewart, 1991).

Although considerable historical and anthropological research
supports the belief that homosexual conduct and identity are socially constructed, there is little contemporary research on the differences between men of color and European-American men regarding the way they integrate self-perceptions of sexual and ethnic
identity into their daily lives. Most current research on homosexually active men does not take race and ethnicity into account. Those
studies that do, tend to focus on some aspect of HIV epidemiology
or prevention such as seroprevalence rates, percentages of men
having sex with other men or engaging in high risk behaviors, or
comparison of sexual behavior and self-identification. To find an
empirical study that compares ethnic groups on the social and psychological variables discussed in this paper, we had to go back to
results reported by Bell and Weinberg (1978) from data collected in
San Francisco between 1970 and 1972.

Consideration of the Bell and Weinberg (1978) study gives rise to
some historical and methodological concerns. First the data are 20
years old, and the intervening years have brought us the gay civil
rights movement and the AIDS epidemic. Both have had a profound
effect on sexual behavior and identity.

Second, the Bell and Weinberg study, like most studies of sexual
minority groups, used recruitment strategies that relied on predominantly European-American gay networks. Participants in these

studies have "tended to be disproportionately white, well educated and middle class, and those few who were less educated or less affluent, or who were members of racial minority groups, were usually attached in some way to members of the majority" (Turner et al., 1989, p. 130).

Johnson (1981) demonstrated the existence of a sub-group of African-American men who had sex with men and remained clearly unattached to the mainstream gay community. He targeted recruitment to two groups of African American men: one that identified primarily as Black and another that identified primarily as gay. He characterized the first group as men who "minimize their involvement with whites and are less open about their homosexuality due to a wide range of factors, one of which appears to be the relative strength of their identification with issues of race over sexual orientation" (p. 4620-B). He concluded that Bell and Weinberg had failed to tap the range of identities that existed among African-American men who have sex with men.

Third, Bell and Weinberg sought out gay men and lesbians living in San Francisco to participate in a social psychological study with the intent of learning more about variations in homosexual conduct, identity, and lifestyle. In contrast, our study invited participation nationwide from "men who have sex with men" who wanted to lower their risks of HIV transmission. Approximately 20 percent of our sample self-identified as bisexual and a handful identified as straight. We recruited men who were concerned about risky sexual behavior and turned away those who did not meet our risk criteria or who were not interested in safer sex counseling. In short, selection processes for the two studies differed substantially. Nevertheless, the Bell and Weinberg data do provide a point of comparison for many of the variables we will examine. See Table 1 for a list of those we have extracted. The original Bell and Weinberg text does not provide tests of statistical significance for the variables we have chosen to present. Significance levels shown in Table 1 are based on contingency table analyses we did using sample size and percent distributions to compute observed frequencies.

African-American participants in the Bell and Weinberg study were significantly younger and less educated than their European-American counterparts. Fewer of them lived alone; and more had a

TABLE 1. Bell and Weinberg (1978): A Comparison of African- and Euro-pean-American Male Respondents

	African American n = 111	European American n = 575
Age		
% 25 or younger[1]	43	24
% 26 to 35	49	25
% 36 to 45	8	26
% 46 plus	10	25
Mean age	27.2	37.0
Level of education completed[2]		
% High school or less	27	25
% Some college	52	33
% College degree or more	21	42
Living situation[2]		
% Alone	29	37
% With same sex roommate	64	50
% Other	7	13
Kinsey Scale[3]		
% Exclusively homosexual - behavior[2]	62	74
% Exclusively homosexual - feelings[2]	45	58
% self-report exclusive homosexuality[2]	41	55
% no regret about being homosexual	59	49
% disagree homosexuality is a disorder	39	43
% most relatives know respondent has sex with men	29	35
% most others know respondent has sex with men	32	33
Proportion of opposite race sex partners[2]		
None	2	22
Half or less	31	78
More than half	67	0
% currently coupled	29	29

[1] Percents are shown as reported in Bell and Weinberg. For African-Americans, they total 110 percent. However, information they provide on the pool of 316 men from which the sample of 111 was drawn, indicates that only one of the potential respondents was age 46 or older. Therefore, rather than 10 percent, no more than 1 percent of the African-American respondents could have been 46 or older. Assuming the other percentages are wrong by no more than 1 percent, African-American respondents in this study were significantly younger (p < .05) than European-American ones.

[2] p < .05

[3] Respondents chose categories on a seven point scale ranging from exclusively heterosexual to exclusively homosexual.

same sex roommate. Fewer African-American respondents identified as exclusively homosexual. Most reported that the majority of their sex partners were European American men. In contrast, all European American respondents said half or fewer of their partners were African-American men. No significant differences were found between the groups in regrets about being homosexual, the belief that homosexuality is a disorder, or in the disclosure of their sexual orientation to relatives and others.

METHODS

The current study draws on information provided by participants in Project ARIES, a safer sex group counseling program for men who have sex with men and want to lower their risk of HIV transmission.

Recruitment

Outreach to potential participants occurred through four venues: stories, and display and classified ads in gay publications; news and feature stories in the mainstream press; personal contacts and quarterly mailings of information and display materials to gay community organizations, public health departments and STD/HIV test sites; and outreach via phone calls and print materials to gay bars and baths. In all, print materials were sent to roughly 2000 organizations.

Because the aim was to recruit men at risk for HIV transmission and not solely those who identified as gay or bisexual, all of the publicity referred to "men who have sex with men" rather than "gay" or "bisexual" men. Efforts to gain coverage in the mainstream press resulted in major newspaper stories in 5 U.S. cities, and a wire service story about the project that was distributed to over 1200 newspapers, television and radio stations.

In an effort to reach men of color, three of the five pieces of artwork used for posters and display ads featured Latino- or African-American men. We also ran one campaign featuring the African-American display ad in papers along the West Coast targeted to communities of color.

All marketing materials prominently featured a toll-free telephone number by which interested persons could contact us. Although targeted recruitment efforts occurred in 8 states, we received phone calls from all 50 states, Puerto Rico and Canada. Over the planned 18 month recruitment period, we received 4,649 calls, an even 2,500 of which were from men interested in the counseling program.

Screening

The initial screening process determined whether the caller was interested in the counseling program and met minimum eligibility criteria. To do so, callers had to be male, 18 years of age or older, and report three or more instances of unprotected oral or anal intercourse with another man in the last three months. Men passing the initial screen proceeded to an intake interview to assess the fit between the services ARIES could offer and those the caller was seeking, and to determine the presence of mental health or substance use issues that would prevent the caller from participating productively in group counseling. Referrals were offered to callers who were seeking some other type of service or were found ineligible.

Baseline Assessment

Approximately two hours of baseline data collection were accomplished in four structured telephone interviews at least a week apart. This was done so that four weeks of sexual activity information could be collected in close proximity to actual events, thus enhancing accuracy of recall while collecting information across an interval sufficiently long to capture some variation in sexual behavior across time. Among other topics, the baseline assessment also collected information on demographics, self-perceived sexual identity, disclosure, social supports, and sexual behavior during the twelve weeks preceding the first interview.

Sample

Recruitment began in April, 1992, and ended in October, 1993. Attrition occurred throughout the pre-counseling process. Out of the 2500 callers seeking counseling, 1720 met the minimum eligibility criteria, 822 completed the clinical intake and 614 began the baseline assessment process. The data presented here are from 513 men who completed the first two baseline assessments and identified their ethnicity as African-, Latino-, or European-American. Data on an additional 25 men from other ethnic groups who completed the first two interviews are excluded because their numbers are too small to permit meaningful statistical comparisons.

RESULTS

As with other studies of homosexually active men (Lever et al., 1992), Project ARIES data are derived from a convenience sample of men who chose to contact the project. Their representativeness of the larger population of homosexually active men is unknown. Comparison with other published studies, however, does provide some context for interpreting the results. Unless otherwise noted, ANOVA was used to test for statistical significance of differences in ethnic group means, and the chi-square statistic was used to test group differences on categorical variables.

Demographics

Like the Bell and Weinberg study, African-American, as well as Latino-American respondents were significantly younger than European-American ones. Unlike Bell and Weinberg's participants, men of color were as well educated as those of European descent. In all three groups, levels of educational attainment were higher than those reported by Bell and Weinberg. In the current study, a significantly higher percentage of African-American respondents were unemployed, retired or disabled than was true for either Latino- or European-American men. However, no significant differences were reported in income levels across the groups. Fewer men of color had never been legally married, but the differences were not statistically significant (see Table 2).

Sexual Identity and Behavior

No statistically significant differences were found between African-, Latino-, and European-American participants with respect to

TABLE 2. Demographic Characteristics of the Sample

	African American n = 31	Latino American n = 38	European American n = 444
Mean age[1]	29.2	30.9	37.2
Mean years of education	15.1	15.3	15.4
Level of education completed			
% High school or less	12.9	15.8	13.7
% Some college	48.4	50.0	34.5
% College degree or more	38.7	34.2	51.8
Current employment status[1]			
% Full - time	51.6	67.6	63.3
% Part - time or occasion	6.5	16.2	16.9
% Unemployed, retired, or disabled	41.9	16.2	19.8
Current or most recent occupation			
% Executive or professional	35.7	44.1	45.7
% Technical, sales, or administrative support	46.4	41.2	30.7
% Service occupations	19.7	8.8	13.8
% Other	-	5.9	9.8
Annual income			
% Under $10,000	25.8	18.4	17.6
% $10,000 to 19,999	16.1	21.1	18.5
% $20,000 to 29,999	25.8	31.6	23.7
% $30,000 to 39,999	16.1	21.1	17.2
% $40,000 to 49,999	9.7	5.3	8.8
% $50,000 or more	6.5	2.6	14.2
Estimated mean income[2]	23,710	23,157	27,370
Marital Status			
% Currently married	3.2	5.3	11.0
% Separated, divorced or widowed	12.9	15.8	19.4
% Never married	83.9	78.9	69.6

[1] $p < .05$

[2] Respondents reported income in ranges of $10,000. This estimate uses the mid-points of the ranges to calculate mean income.

their sexual identity and sexual partners. Additionally, as with Bell and Weinberg's findings, ARIES respondents reported generally positive attitudes toward having sex with men and there were no statistically significant differences among ethnic groups with respect to personal acceptance of homosexual behavior (see Table 3).

TABLE 3. Sexual Identity and Sexual Partners

	African American n = 31	Latino American n = 38	European American n = 444
Sexual orientation self-label			
% Gay/homosexual	80.6	76.3	79.7
% Bisexual	16.1	23.7	19.1
% Straight/heterosexual	3.2	-	1.1
Kinsey Scale[1]			
% Exclusively homosexual - behavior	61.3	60.5	67.8
% Exclusively homosexual - feelings	54.8	52.6	51.8
% Exclusively homosexual - both	48.8	47.4	47.5
% Sex with a woman in the past year	22.6	21.1	20.5
Mean number of male partners in the past year	35.5	37.6	52.1
Mean number of female partners in the past year[2]	4.5	1.6	3.5
Frequency of sex with male vs. female partners[2]			
% More often with men than with women	71.4	62.5	72.5
% About equally with men and women	28.6	25.0	12.1
% More often with women than men	-	12.5	14.2
Attitudes towards having sex with men[3]			
Easy to accept that I have sex with men	3.6	3.5	3.4
Comfortable with fact of having sex with men	3.5	3.3	3.3
Wish I weren't attracted to men	2.0	1.8	1.9
Sex with men is a positive expression of sexuality	3.4	3.4	3.4
I feel internal conflict over having sex with men	2.1	2.0	2.1
I don't think of myself as being gay	1.8	1.6	1.7

[1] Respondents chose categories on a seven point scale ranging from exclusively homosexual to exclusively heterosexual.

[2] Based on 7 African-, 8 Latino- and 91 European-American men who reported sex wtih a woman in the past year.

[3] Table shows group means on a scale that ranges from 1 = Strongly disagree to 4 = Strongly agree.

TABLE 3. (cont.)

	African American n = 31	Latino American n = 38	European American n = 444
I enjoy spending time with gay men	3.2	3.2	3.2
It's easy for me to accept that I'm ___ [4]	3.3	3.2	3.2
Being ___ makes me part of a community	2.6	2.8	2.7
Being ___ is central to how I think about myself	2.7	2.9	2.9
I'm glad I'm ___	3.0	3.0	3.0

[4] This set of statements used the terms "gay" or "bisexual" depending on the respondents' self-labeling. Six men, one African- and five European-Americans, identified as "straight" and were not asked these questions.

Bell and Weinberg found that a larger percentage of European-American than African American men self-identified as exclusively homosexual. In contrast, ARIES data indicate no difference in the proportion of men from each group who identified themselves as gay or homosexual. Furthermore, no differences were found in the proportion of men who described themselves, behaviorally or in terms of feelings, as exclusively gay. Over 60 percent of the men in each racial category reported exclusive homosexual behavior and over 50 percent reported exclusive homosexual feelings.

Most empirical evidence, including data from the U.S. Centers for Disease Control (CDC), points to a significantly higher incidence of bisexual behavior among men of color (Chu et al., 1992; Diaz et al., 1993; Doll et al., 1991; Doll et al., 1992). It is noteworthy, however, that the CDC AIDS case report data classify as bisexual men who report *any* sex with both men and women since 1978. Of the 7,358 AIDS cases among men who had sex with men reported to the CDC for the year ending June 30, 1993, a total of 19.0 percent were among men classified as bisexual. By ethnic group, the figures were 28.4 percent for African-Americans, 23.1 for Latino-Americans, and 14.6 percent for European-Americans. Because ARIES respondents reported on only one year of behavior and CDC data covered the preceding 15 years, it is logical to anticipate that CDC data would include a higher proportion of "bisexual" men than the ARIES sample. This expectation held for the men of color, but the proportion of European-American ARIES partici-pants whose behavior or identity was bisexual surpassed that of the CDC data.

Across ethnic groups, ARIES respondents reported about the same overall level of bisexual conduct and identity. About one fifth of the men in each of the three groups reported having sex with a woman in the past year, and similar proportions self-identified as bisexual. Between 29 and 37 percent reported they had sex with women at least as often as with men. Only a handful of men re-ported they were heterosexual.

Social Support

Table 4 provides data, by ethnic group, for a number of variables related to social support. Some apparent differences exist in the living arrangements of men in the study, however, the numbers of African and Latino-Americans are too small to test for statistical significance. Unlike the Bell and Weinberg sample, living alone was the single most common arrangement among all three groups, and predominated among European-American men. Among all three groups, a sizable number were living either with male lovers or roommates, but the proportions did not reach the levels Bell and Weinberg reported. In contrast to a small proportion of European-American men, approximately one quarter of the men of color were living with non-spousal relatives. It is also noteworthy that a nu-merical minority of respondents, mostly European-American, were living with spouses. These familial living arrangements may have affected respondents' access to privacy for their participation in ARIES interviews and group sessions.

There were no ethnic differences in the prevalence of primary relationships with male partners, nor in the length of those relation-ships. However, echoing the pattern Bell and Weinberg found among male sex partners, European-American men were more like-ly to report a primary partner from their same ethnic group than either African or Latino-American respondents. In contrast, among the few men who reported primary female partners, homogeneity of ethnicity was the norm in all three groups.

Disclosure plays an important role in the process of garnering social support. Without disclosure, gaining support from others,

TABLE 4. Social Supports

	African American n = 31	Latino American n = 38	European American n = 444
Living situation			
% Alone	45.2	45.9	52.6
% With male lover	16.1	5.4	10.8
% With wife	3.2	2.7	9.5
% With other adult relative	25.8	27.0	7.7
% With friend, roommate	9.7	18.9	17.4
% Other	-	-	2.0
% In primary relationship with a man	29.0	13.2	21.5
Mean length of relationship (months)[1]	32.8	37.4	51.2
% Same ethnic group as primary male partner[1]	22.2	0	86.5
% In primary relationship with a woman	3.2	8.1	10.9
% Same ethnic group as primary female partner[2]	100.0	66.7	93.6
Disclosure to others			
% who are more than half "out of the closet"	51.6	62.2	55.6
% out to more than half of closest friends	77.4	81.6	72.5
% out to more than half of casual friends	45.2	57.9	50.1
% out to more than half of closest co-workers	27.6	43.2	34.9
% out to at least one parent	70.0	65.8	64.8
% out to at least one sibling	65.5	80.6	66.2
Mean family acceptance of their sex with men[3]	2.8	2.6	2.6
Mean friends' acceptance of their sex with men[3]	4.1	4.0	3.8
Mean self-acceptance of their sex with men[3]	4.3	4.2	4.2

[1] Based on primary male relationships reported by 9 African-, 5 Latino- and 95 European-American men.

[2] Based on primary female relationships reported by 1 African-, 3 Latino- and 48 European-American men.

[3] Table shows mean scores based on a scale that ranges from 1 = Not at all to 5 = Extremely accepting.

TABLE 4. (cont.)

	African American n = 31	Latino American n = 38	European American n = 444
Number of different gay-oriented activities			
Political[4]	1.7	2.4	2.1
Social[5]	1.6	1.7	1.6
Going to gay bars or gay baths[6]	1.4	1.6	1.4

[4] Includes 4 activities: donating money to gay causes, volunteering time to gay causes, participating in gay marches and wearing gay buttons.
[5] Includes 3 activities: participating in organized gay social activites, attending gay counseling or support groups, and attending gay cultural events.
[6] These are counted as 2 activities.

particularly with regard to sexual issues, is difficult. Fifty-six percent of Project ARIES participants described themselves mostly "out of the closet." Across ethnic groups, about two-thirds were "out" to at least one parent. On average, men were least likely to disclose in the workplace. Although none of the differences reached statistical significance, Latino-Americans tended to be the least closeted. It appears that ARIES respondents in all three ethnic groups were less closeted than the men Bell and Weinberg interviewed 20 years ago.

There were no differences across groups with regard to perceived acceptance of sexual behavior by others. In all ethnic groups, the men reported that family members were comparatively less accepting of their sexual behavior than friends. Paired t-tests revealed this difference was statistically significant ($p < .001$) in all three groups. African- and Latino-American men reported no difference between friends' acceptance of their sexual behavior and their own acceptance. However, European-American men rated their self-acceptance as significantly higher than perceived acceptance by their friends (paired t-test, $p < .001$).

To examine integration into the gay community, respondents were presented with a list of gay-oriented activities and asked to indicate the ones they had participated in during the last five years. Activities were grouped into three categories: political, social, and going to bars and baths. The results presented in Table 4 represent the number of types of activities reported and not the extent of participation. Latino-American men report a larger array of political activities than African- and European-American men, a difference that approaches statistical significance. There were no between group differences in participation in social activities or in patronizing gay bars and baths.

Social Networks

Here we leave the path forged by Bell and Weinberg and break new ground. We asked participants to think about the six most important adults in their lives and to respond to a series of questions about each of them. Those who chose to name fewer than six persons were allowed to do so.

For each individual named, we asked respondents to identify the individual's gender, ethnicity, sexual orientation, knowledge of the respondent's sexual behavior, whether they had discussed safer sex with the individual, and the extent to which the individual was or would be accepting of the respondent's homosexual behavior.

For each respondent we computed a single aggregate score for each network variable. For dichotomous variables we calculated the percent of the network that was (1) male; (2) from the respondent's ethnic group; (3) gay, lesbian or bisexual, etc. Perceived acceptance of respondent's homosexual behavior had been measured on a five point scale, and we used the mean of the individual ratings as the respondent's network score. Averages of these composite scores were then calculated for each ethnic group, and are presented in the first section of Table 5.

No significant differences were found between groups in the percentages of networks that were male, sexual minorities, knew the respondent had sex with men, had discussed issues of sexual safety with the respondent, or in their perceived acceptance of the respondent's sexual behavior. Ethnic composition of the networks, however, did vary dramatically. On average, the social networks of the African- and Latino-American men were significantly more ethnically diverse than those of the European-American respondents.

To examine this difference more closely, the second section of Table 5 provides information on the ethnic composition of individual networks. Approximately three-quarters of European-American

TABLE 5. Social Network Characteristics

	African American n = 31	Latino American n = 37[1]	European American n = 444
Six most important adults in respondents' lives			
Mean % who are male	60.0	62.3	60.6
Mean % from the same ethnic group[2]	64.5	62.9	92.4
Mean % who are also gay or bisexual	40.3	46.9	44.6
Mean % who know they have sex with men	74.7	77.8	78.5
Mean % with whom they discuss sexual safety	65.3	71.7	63.2
Mean acceptance of their sex with men[3]	3.7	3.8	3.8
% of respondents whose networks include no one from their own ethnic group	16.1	2.7	0
% of respondents whose networks are ethnically diverse	48.4	78.4	27.5
% of respondents whose networks include no one from other ethnic groups	35.5	18.9	72.5
% of respondents whose networks include no one who is gay or bisexual	12.9	10.8	13.3
% of respondents whose networks include gay or bisexual and straight persons	80.6	78.4	77.8
% of respondents whose networks include solely gay or bisexual persons	6.5	10.8	7.9

[1]Network variables are missing for one Latino-American respondent.
[2]$p < .05$
[3]Table shows mean scores based on a scale that ranges from 1 = Not at all to 5 = Extremely accepting.

respondents had networks comprised entirely of other European-American persons. The remainder had networks that included persons of color. No European-American men had networks comprised entirely of persons from other ethnic groups. This pattern differs sharply from that observed among African- and Latino-American men. Sixteen percent of African-American men had networks comprised entirely of persons from other ethnic groups. Thirty-five percent had networks that were solely African-American, and nearly half reported networks that were ethnically diverse. Fully 78 percent of the Latino-American respondents reported that their networks were ethnically diverse. Only one person reported his network included no Latino/Latinas, and only 19 percent reported networks that were exclusively Latino-American.

The third section of Table 5 presents parallel analyses for the sexual minority composition of respondents' networks. No ethnic differences were found. Across all three ethnic groups, approximately 80 percent of respondents' networks were comprised of a mix of sexual minority and heterosexual persons; upwards of 10 percent mentioned no other sexual minorities in their networks; and the networks of the remaining respondents were exclusively gay, lesbian, and bisexual.

For the next set of analyses (Table 6), we subdivided network members into two groups, those of the same ethnic group as the respondent and those from a different one. For each sub-group, we computed the mean percent who were gay, lesbian or bisexual, who knew the respondent had sex with men, and who had discussed safer sex with the respondent. We also computed mean acceptance scores for each sub-group.

Results were consistent for all three groups of respondents. Network members whose ethnicity differed from that of the respondent were, on average, more likely to be gay, lesbian or bisexual themselves, were more likely to know the respondent had sex with men, were more likely to have discussed issues of sexual safety with the respondent, and were perceived as more accepting of the respondent's having sex with men. Given the perception of homophobia among African- and Latino-American communities, these results are not too surprising. What was unexpected, however, was that the pattern also held for European-American men.

These results suggested that shared sexual inclinations were serving as a bridge across ethnic boundaries. To test this hypothesis, we regressed the network sexual orientation and ethnicity variables on perceived network acceptance. We used hierarchical regression, entering the sexual orientation variable first. We did this to test whether ethnic composition of the networks would explain any

TABLE 6. Sexual Orientation of, Disclosure to, Acceptance by, and Safer Sex Discussions with Network Members, Controlling for Their Ethnicity

	African American n = 31	Latino American n = 37	European American n = 444
Mean % who are gay, lesbian or bisexual			
Same ethnic group	31.0	37.0	41.7
Different ethnic group	62.9	74.4	68.1
Mean % who know respondent has sex with men			
Same ethnic group	72.4	74.8	75.7
Different ethnic group	79.2	90.5	87.9
Mean % with whom respondent has discussed safer sex			
Same ethnic group	53.7	67.0	61.6
Different ethnic group	87.5	90.5	81.4
Mean acceptance of respondent's sex with men			
Same ethnic group	3.0	3.5	3.6
Different ethnic group	4.4	4.5	4.5

variance in the likelihood of perceived acceptance by network members once the effects of their sexual orientation were removed. We then reversed the order of entry for the independent variables to see whether results would be substantially affected. They were not. Results of the first set of regressions are presented in Table 7.

Among each of the ethnic groups, the regression equation explained a significant amount of variance in perceived acceptance among network members. For Latino- and European-American respondents, all of the explained variance was accounted for by the percent of network members who were gay, lesbian, or bisexual. Removing the effects of network members' sexual orientation, their ethnicity added nothing more to the explanation of variation in perceived network acceptance among Latino- and European-American participants. These results support the hypothesis that, for these groups, shared sexual minority status and not perceived homophobia among members of their own ethnic group accounts for the greater acceptance Latino- and European-American respondents reported among network members from other ethnic groups.

Among African-American men, the percent of the network that was gay, lesbian, or bisexual also explained a significant, though

TABLE 7. Sexual Orientation and Ethnicity of Network Members as Predictors of Perceived Acceptance

African-American Men, n = 31

Variable	b	se (b)	Beta	Sig.
% network gay, lesbian, bisexual	.016	.006	.410	.011
% network same ethnic group as respondent	−.011	.004	− .393	.014
Constant	3.736	.415		
Total adjusted R²				.33

Latino-American Men, n = 37

Variable	b	se (b)	Beta	Sig.
% network gay, lesbian, bisexual	.025	.005	.710	.000
% network same ethnic group as respondent	.000	.005	.027	.836
Constant	2.514	.447		
Total adjusted R²				.46

European-American Men, n = 444

Variable	b	se (b)	Beta	Sig.
% network gay, lesbian, bisexual	.022	.001	.616	.000
% network same ethnic group as respondent	.000	.002	− .013	.726
Constant	2.815	.223		
Total adjusted R²				.38

smaller, portion of variance in perceived network acceptance. However, the effects of ethnic composition of the network were also significant. For African-American men who have sex with men, it appears that perceived network acceptance is positively linked to the proportion of network members who are also gay, lesbian or bisexual, and negatively linked to the proportion who are African-American.

We would expect the presence of network members who are themselves African-American and gay, lesbian or bisexual would be positively associated with perceived network acceptance. It is, but the relationship is weak (r = .13). This is likely due to the fact not many such persons were part of the respondents' networks. Forty-two percent of respondents named no network members who shared both their ethnicity and sexual orientation, 26 percent named only one such person and only a third named more than one.

DISCUSSION

Although there are some significant ethnic differences, the overall impression is one of general similarity across African-, Latino- and European-American men participating in Project ARIES. Although men of color are younger and although African-American men are more likely to be unemployed, retired or disabled, the men are similar in their educational background and income. No important differences were discovered with regard to sexual identity and behavior and social support. In all three groups, substantial proportions of the men are gay-identified, content with their sexuality, active in the gay community, and out to friends and family. With regard to social network there are also few differences. No ethnic differences were found in the percentages of networks that were male and gay, lesbian or bisexual. Similarly, social network members were equally likely to know about and accept the homosexual behavior of the respondent.

When differences are present they appear to indicate that sexual identity and behavior act as integrating mechanisms into the larger gay community. African- and Latino-American men are significantly more likely than European-American men to report they are coupled with–or friends with–persons from ethnic groups other than their own. Network ethnic diversity, when built around sexual orientation, significantly accounts for the acceptance all men perceive in their network.

The analyses of the social networks of African-American men lend modest empirical support to the observation that African-American men who have sex with men are hard pressed to find acceptance that is uncompromised by homophobia or racism. Among their most intimate friends and relations, most African-American respondents report no more than one person who is also African-American and lesbian, gay or bisexual. A few report networks in which no one shares their ethnicity. We have no data on the extent to which our respondents perceive the gay community to be racist. However, those with greater numbers of African-Americans in their social networks are more likely to report lower perceived acceptance of their homosexual behavior.

The data presented here are compiled from a relatively small, convenience sample. Because of this limitation we must be cautious in interpreting the results. Like other studies, men of color in the present study may be disproportionately represented by individuals who are well-integrated into the predominantly European-American gay culture. Thus, the findings may not be generalizeable to the universe of African- and Latino-American men who have sex with other men.

The absence of an ethnic difference in the proportion of men who identify as bisexual or straight may indicate some differential success in recruiting non-gay-identified men. Comparison with CDC AIDS case report data, in which higher proportions of men of color and fewer European-American men are classified as bisexual, suggests that Project ARIES was more successful in recruiting non-gay-identified participants among men of European descent than among men of color.

This may be so in spite of Project ARIES' commitment to reach out beyond the gay community to the non-gay identified. If this is the case, outreach strategies to homosexually active men of color need to be rethought. Since previous research suggests that a large number of men of color are homosexually active but not gay identified, other vehicles for offering services to this population are necessary.

One approach that has met with some success is to locate HIV prevention services within agencies based in communities of color. An acknowledged limitation of such services has been the reluctance of some community residents to disclose their risk behaviors by virtue of coming forward for services. We believe the ARIES experience demonstrates the feasibility of delivering anonymous services via the telephone, and would encourage agencies serving communities of color to consider the telephone as a means for reaching individuals who do not wish to disclose their identity.

Although the results may not be generalizeable, they likely reflect an important reality that is often overlooked. Most who write on ethnic sensitivity caution that as many within group as between group differences exist. Service providers should not assume therefore that all men of color are the same and that they are in all ways different from men of European descent. The results here indicate that a significant, although unknown, number of homosexually active men of color are not very different from white gay men. Substantial numbers of men of color are likely to be gay identified and to participate in the larger gay community, including those social services and activities designed for the gay community. The results also suggest that sexual identity can be as central to one's sense of self as ethnic identity. Those men of color who come to recognize their homosexual interest or experience discrimination within their own communities are likely to seek a niche within the larger gay community. The results here suggest that many do find their niche and with it a greater sense of social acceptance.

Future research needs to be aimed at understanding as wide a range of homosexually active men of color as possible. It may be that studies using non-probability samples are inadequate to this task. Joseph Harry (1990) has argued that random sampling techniques can be used to study sexual identity and conduct. Examining a Roper poll, he argues that gay men will not only self-identify but will not look like the profile suggested by non-random samples of gay men. A recent Yankelovich Monitors survey, which tracks consumer attitudes using random sampling techniques, uncovered 5.7% who described themselves as "gay/homosexual/lesbian" (Elliott, 1994). It is not unreasonable to assume that surveys using questions that ask for behavior as well as identity can elicit a larger percentage who are homosexually active even if not gay identified. Adding survey techniques that oversample for race and ethnicity would enable us to develop a more accurate understanding of men (and women) of color.

NOTE

This research was funded by the National Institute of Mental Health, grant number RO1-MH46792. We wish to thank several individuals for their contributions to this paper. Alex Riggle and Sharon Hopkins from the Seattle-King County Department of Public Health provided data from the Center for Disease Control AIDS Surveillance data set. Mary Gillmore and Larry Icard of the University of

Washington School of Social Work reviewed earlier drafts of the manuscript. Finally, we are indebted to Jeffrey Kelly and his colleagues for permitting us to adopt the Project ARIES name which they had created for their pioneering AIDS prevention intervention.

REFERENCES

Beame, T. (1982). Young, gifted, Black and gay: Dr. Julius Johnson. *Advocate, 346*, 25-27, 55.

Bell, A., & Weinberg, M. (1978). *Homosexualities: A study of diversity among men and women.* New York: Simon & Schuster.

Chu, S., Peterman, T., Doll, L., Buehler, J., & Curran, J. (1992). AIDS in bisexual men in the United States: Epidemiology and transmission to women. *American Journal of Public Health, 82*(2), 220-224.

DeMarco, J. (1983). Gay racism. In M. Smith (Ed.), *Black men/white men: A gay anthology* (pp. 109-118). San Francisco: Gay Sunshine Press.

Diaz, T., Chu, S., Frederick, M., Hermann, P., Levy, A., Mokotoff, E., Whyte, B., Conti, L., Herr, M., Checko, P., Rietmeijer, C., Sorvillo, F., & Quaiser, M. (1993). Sociodemographics and HIV risk behaviors of bisexual men with AIDS: Results from a multistate interview project. *AIDS, 7*(9), 1227-1232.

Doll, L., Byers, R., Bolan, G., Douglas, J., Moss, P., Weller, P., Joy, D., Bartholow, B., & Harrison, J. (1991). Homosexual men who engage in high-risk sexual behavior. *Sexually Transmitted Diseases, 18*(3), 170-175.

Doll, L., Petersen, L., White, C., Johnson, E., & Ward, J. (1992). Homosexually and nonhomosexually identified men who have sex with men: A behavioral comparison. *Journal of Sex Research, 29*(1), 1-14.

Elliott, S. (1994). A sharper view of gay consumers. *New York Times*, June 9, 1994. pp. C1,4.

Ernst, F., Francis, R., Nevels, H., & Lemeh, C. (1991). Condemnation of homosexuality in the Black community: A gender-specific phenomenon? *Archives of Sexual Behavior, 20*(6), 579-585.

Green, J. (1982). *Cultural awareness in the human services.* Englewood Cliffs, NJ: Prentice-Hall.

Harry, J. (1990). A probability sample of gay males. *Journal of Homosexuality, 19*(1), 89-104.

Icard, L. (1986). Black gay men and conflicting social identities: Sexual orientation versus racial identity. In J. Gripton & M. Valentich (Eds.), *Social work practice in sexual problems* (pp. 83-93). New York: The Haworth Press, Inc.

Icard, L., Schilling, R., El Bassel, N., & Young, D. (1992). Preventing AIDS among Black gay men and Black gay and heterosexual male intravenous drug users. *Social Work, 37*(5), 440-445.

Johnson, J. (1982). Influence of assimilation on the psychosocial adjustment of black homosexual men. *Dissertation Abstracts International, 42*(11), 4620-B.

Klein, F., Sepekoff, B., & Wolf, T. (1985). Sexual orientation: A multi-variable dynamic process. *Journal of Homosexuality, 11*(1-2), 35-49.

Lever, J., Kanouse, D., Rogers, W., Carson, S., & Hertz, R. (1992). Behavior patterns and sexual identity of bisexual men. *Journal of Sex Research, 29*(2), 141-167.

Loiacano, D. (1989). Gay identity development issues among Black Americans: Racism, homophobia, and the need for validation. *Journal of Counseling and Development, 68*(1), 21-25.

Longres, J. (1991). Toward a status model of ethnic sensitive practice. *Journal of Multicultural Social Work, 1*(1), 41-56.

Magaña, J., & Carrier, J. (1991). Mexican and Mexican American male sexual behavior and spread of AIDS in California. *Journal of Sex Research, 28*(3), 425-441.

Marín, G. (1989). AIDS prevention among Hispanics: Needs, risk behaviors, and cultural values. *Public Health Reports, 104*(5), 411-415.

Marlatt, G., & Gordon, J. (1985). *Relapse prevention.* New York: Guilford Press.

Peterson, J., & Marín, G. (1988). Issues in the prevention of AIDS among Black and Hispanic men. *American Psychologist, 43*(11), 871-877.

Prochaska, J., & DiClemente, C. (1983). Stages and processes of self-change of smoking: Toward an integrative model of change. *Journal of Consulting and Clinical Psychology, 51*, 390-395.

Singer, M., Flores, C., Davison, L., Burke, G., Castillo, Z., Scanlon, K., & Rivera, M. (1990). SIDA: The economic, social, and cultural context of AIDS among Latinos. *Medical Anthropology Quarterly, 4*(1), 72-114.

Stewart, C. (1991). Black, gay (and invisible)–double jeopardy. *New Republic, 205*(23), 13-15.

Turner, C., Miller, H., & Moses, L. (1989). *AIDS: sexual behavior and intravenous drug use.* Washington, D.C.: National Academy Press.

Assessing the Psychosocial Well-Being of African American Gays: A Multidimensional Perspective

Larry D. Icard

SUMMARY. This paper presents a model for assessing personal, cultural, and social factors influencing the psychosocial well-being of black gay men. Differences are discussed by focusing on three groups–adolescent, adult and older gay African American men. Each of these groups is considered in connection with the developmental tasks of play, work and love. These tasks are explored as a function of age cohort, gender appearances, socioeconomic status, church and religion, and area of residence as they are linked to an individual's participation in the black, gay, and black gay communities. These intersecting domains are addressed within the context of racism as they affect the psychosocial well-being of black gay men. *[Article copies available from The Haworth Document Delivery Service: 1-800-342-9678. E-mail address: getinfo@haworth.com]*

In spite of an increasing emphasis on gay issues, relatively little attention has been given to African American gay men. The aim of this paper therefore is to further our understanding by outlining a model for assessing their psychosocial well-being and service

Larry D. Icard, DSW, is Associate Professor, University of Washington, School of Social Work, Seattle, WA 98195.

[Haworth co-indexing entry note]: "Assessing the Psychosocial Well-Being of African American Gays: A Multidimensional Perspective." Icard, Larry D. Co-published simultaneously in *Journal of Gay & Lesbian Social Services* (The Haworth Press, Inc.) Vol. 5, No. 2/3, 1996, pp. 25-49; and: *Men of Color: A Context for Service to Homosexually Active Men* (ed: John F. Longres) The Haworth Press, Inc., 1996, pp. 25-49; and: *Men of Color: A Context for Service to Homosexually Active Men* (ed: John F. Longres) Harrington Park Press, an imprint of The Haworth Press, Inc., 1996, pp. 25-49. Single or multiple copies of this article are available from The Haworth Document Delivery Service [1-800-342-9678, 9:00 a.m. - 5:00 p.m. (EST). E-mail address: getinfo@haworth.com].

25

needs. The model calls attention to the need to distinguish among three age cohorts–those who are presently adolescents, adults, or older adults. The early life socialization of each of these has taken place during distinct historical periods so that their psychosocial development and ways of interacting are quite different. The paper begins with a review of the literature on African American gays. The assessment model is then presented followed by a discussion highlighting issues relating to race and racism, age cohort, physical appearance and mannerisms, socio-economic status, urban-rural residence, religion, and family and community as reference groups.

AFRICAN AMERICAN GAYS: LITERATURE REVIEW

Until recently, information on African American gays was limited to studies comparing black-white differences (Bell & Weinberg, 1978; Kinsey, Pomeroy & Martin, 1948). In 1981 Johnson signaled a change by focusing exclusively on self-identified African American gay men, thereby understanding them in their own light. He described two groups of men–"gay black" and "black gay," depending upon whether their normative information and social support derived primarily from the gay as opposed to the African American community.

Following Johnson's (1981) work, theoretical discussion focused on understanding the negative emotional consequences resulting from the somewhat opposing norms and expectations placed on African American men by these two communities. In particular, the African American community expects men to marry, have children, and put aside any homosexual desires while the gay community encourages the open acknowledgement of homosexual conduct and identity. The conflict caused by these competing expectations may contribute to a wide range of pathogenic conduct including substance abuse and AIDS risk behavior (Icard & Traunstein, 1987; Icard, Schilling, El-Bassel, & Young, 1992).

Further insights on the importance of the black and gay communities' social support for the well-being of black gays are provided through Loiacano's (1989) interviews with a small sample of African American gays and lesbians. More recently, Peterson and his colleagues (1992) found that many African American men who engage in repeated same sex relations do not identify themselves as gay but rather as heterosexual. Peterson's findings underscore the necessity of distinguishing between African American men who engage in same sex behavior from gay identified African American men.

Although research on African American gay men continues to progress, at least three limitations emerge from reviewing the literature. One, attention seems centered on young adults. For instance, the average age of the gay black men in Bell and Weinberg's (1978) study was 25 years. Other studies have also focused on gay African Americans between the ages of 20 and 40 (Mays et al., 1992; Peterson et al., 1992; Icard & Traunstein, 1987; Icard, Schilling, El-Bassel, & Young, 1992). Although Berger (1982, 1984) and Berger and Kelly (1986) studied gay men over forty, their samples did not include African Americans. Likewise, although studies have begun to raise concern about adolescents (Herdt & Boxer, 1993), information on gay African American youth is limited.

Second, more than ten years have passed since Johnson's breakthrough study distinguishing black gays and gay blacks. Since that time an African American gay sub-community (to be subsequently discussed) has emerged requiring us to refine our understanding of homosexual identity among African Americans. Third, the study of gay African Americans has emphasized the negative aspects of their lives. Much of the recent literature has been directed at understanding substance abuse and unsafe sex practices. There is need therefore for information on the positive circumstances of gay African Americans.

TOWARD AN ASSESSMENT FRAMEWORK

Being able to pose appropriate questions and interpret their responses is fundamental to providing good service. Toward this end, this article outlines a framework for developing a balanced assessment of young, adult and older adult gay African American men. This framework recognizes that human behavior is multifaceted and that gay African Americans are a diverse population. A primary task in designing services is to identify the obstacles to healthy functioning and build on the strengths in order to facilitate social functioning. The framework urges social workers to collect and organize information on the experiences of black gay men as influenced by multiple social, cultural, psychological, and physiological domains. It also urges that attention be given to the way racism fundamentally affects the lives of African American men.

The model as represented in Figure 1 identifies psychosocial well-being through an individual's ability to perform three fundamental developmental tasks–play, work and love. A black gay's ability to carry out these developmental tasks is viewed as a function of resources and obstacles as mediated through his participation in reference groups. The dynamic interplay between social, cultural, and personal factors distinguishing the black gay individual and his social environment, i.e., age cohort, gender behavior and mannerisms, socio-economic status, education, religion, and urban/rural residence, act as determinants of his reference group identification. The characteristics of a black gay's reference groups therefore significantly influence what he experiences as obstacles and resources in functioning as a black man who is gay. These interacting assessment domains must be viewed within the context of the racism that permeates American society.

Although assessment involves examining the complex interaction among these dimensions, the following discussion will focus on explicating the dimensions separately, identifying some relevant considerations within them, and exploring possible interactive links among them. There is nothing inherent in this framework that limits its application for understanding the life situations of black gay men. The value of the model as a tool for assessing the service needs of black gays lies in its emphasis on the interaction among personal characteristics (age, values, socioeconomic status), black cultural values, institutional and individual racism, and reference groups (attitudes and characteristics of the black, gay, and black gay communities) as they relate to the individual's psychosocial functioning as a homosexual. We consider understanding the relationship among these factors in the context of the developmental tasks of work, play and love important for recognizing the diversity and subsequently the diverse service needs among black gay men.

PSYCHOSOCIAL WELL-BEING

The model is designed to enable social service workers to assess the well-being of African American gay men. The position taken here is that well-being is largely a function of individual values and individual self-perceptions. Following Ginsberg (1955) we do not define well-being as the absence of mental illness or disorder but rather in terms of self-recognized happiness, success, and maturity. When individuals have mastered their environment and come to

FIGURE 1. The Black Gay Male and His Psychosocial Well-Being: A Multi-dimensional Assessment Framework

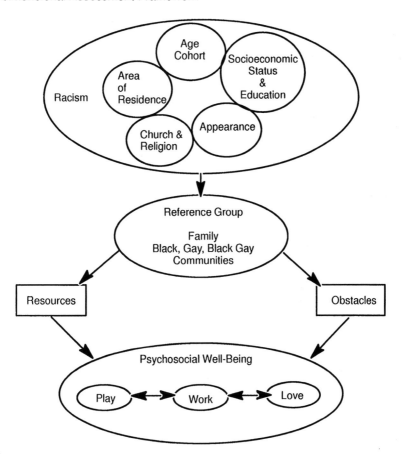

think of themselves as happy, successful, and mature they are mentally healthy. A black gay's perceived well-being may be studied by examining his attitudes on happiness, success, and maturity as these three indicators of psychosocial well-being relate to the developmental tasks of play, work and love.

Play

Play refers to happiness and the ability to have fun through leisure time activities, including the exploration of sexual desires and participation in friendship and family networks. Happiness is an important factor in psychosocial well-being. Huizinga (1955) notes that one of the attributes of play is the ability to feel that one is not participating in "real life," that one is pretending. Play for many African American gay men includes participating in social clubs, fraternal organizations, gay and heterosexual bars, and house parties. It may also include participating in singing groups and church-related activities. Sexual activity is also central to play and the ability of African American gay men to date, and feel attractive and desirable is fundamental to their well-being. Psychosocial well-being may be compromised, however, when constantly cruising for sex becomes the primary leisure time activity. It may also be compromised when leisure activities require suppressing one's sexuality. Research shows that same sex friendships are important for the mental health of a gay person (Cass, 1979; Paul, Weinrich, Gonsiorek, & Hotvedt, 1982). How black gays incorporate heterosexuals into their leisure time therefore is also an important issue. Psychosocial well-being can be jeopardized when African American gays constantly surround themselves with heterosexual friends who do not allow them to openly acknowledge their sexuality.

Work

Work refers to the ability to maintain a livelihood. African American men often define work success in terms of the level of public exposure an occupation provides, the gender-related norms and expectations associated with the occupation, and the monetary rewards. In other words, African American men are likely to feel successful when they are working in traditionally male occupations that provide public visibility or fame, and monetary reward. Social service professionals need to be concerned with the relationship between the psychosocial well-being of a black gay man, the gender appropriateness of his job, the level of fame or public exposure attached to the job, and the amount of monetary reward that he receives for his services.

Love

Love refers to strong feelings of emotional attachment and commitment in an enduring sexual relationship. The ability to experience love is to an extent a function of age. Adolescents may experience mixed emotions and the need for sex may be confused with the need for friendship and intimacy. Emotionally mature adult men should be able to distinguish sex from love and to give of themselves in a committed relationship. Cultural values can play an important role in an African American gay man's ability to love another man. African American values on masculinity hinder the ability of some black gay men to enter loving same sex relationships. Cultural values may cause some black gay men to confuse loving relationships in terms of gender roles. This can result in expecting a partner to take on a feminine or masculine role. During an assessment we therefore need to consider such issues as: (1) the person's values on intimacy with another man; and (2) how cultural gender expectations may influence the person's self-perceptions of being in a mature adult same sex loving relationship.

In addition to work, play and love there is an overarching mental health issue that needs to be assessed. For African American gay men, satisfaction with self also involves the integration of their racial and sexual identities. As a result black gay men are continually caught up in a struggle to reach a satisfactory definition of self, one that integrates these major social identity elements. The integration of self and achieving psychosocial well-being through work, play and love is not simply a function of an individual's abilities. In the next sections, the social and cultural context associated with the struggle for well-being will be analyzed.

RACE AND RACISM

Race and racism are key factors related to the adaptations and social adjustments of African American men regardless of their sexual orientation. African Americans live in a hostile environment (Chestang, 1980) which seriously impinges on their ability to form friendships and intimate relationships and to succeed economically. In spite of gains brought by the civil rights movement, African Americans continue to experience hostile attitudes and limited economic and social opportunities. African Americans experience high rates of unemployment and poverty. They are largely excluded from the housing opportunities other Americans take for granted and as a result are often constrained to neighborhoods where crime, drug abuse, and other social problems are rampant. Such neighborhoods are not conducive to building friendship and support among homosexually oriented men.

The black community offers a nurturing environment (Gary, 1978), a respite from the daily reminder of racism. It facilitates the development of a positive sense of self and offers the possibility for a healthy identity and personality. The black community is not only important during the early formative stages of life but continues to provide protection against racism for adult and older adult African Americans. With regard to homosexual conduct and identity, however, the black community can be less nurturing. African American men are strongly expected to procreate the race and follow heterosexual cultural expectations (Cunningham, 1993; hooks, 1992; Staples, 1982). Yet, African Americans vary in the degree to which they hold homophobic attitudes. Tolerance of homosexuality may be associated with socioeconomic status and education, as it is more apparent among middle class blacks and those working in fields like entertainment and the fashion industry, where homosexuality is generally an openly acknowledged and acceptable lifestyle (Clatterbaugh, 1990).

Many African American gays experience the black community as a homophobic environment (Poussaint, 1990; Stewart, 1991). Some seek validation of their sexuality by fulfilling their needs for play and love through their involvement in the gay community. Such a step raises the possibility for African American gays to experience racism in the gay community while negating the support that would ordinarily be available to them through the black community. In such instances, the black gay's psychosocial well-being is seriously threatened by the discordance occurring between one's sexuality and one's racial identity. Furthermore, the individual's ability to effectively meet the developmental task of work may be compromised by the constraints he experiences in attempting to fulfill his needs for play and love.

Some black gays rely on the black community to meet their needs for play and love. The negative attitudes held by many African Americans may result in these men highly compartmentalizing their homosexuality to reduce the possibility of their being ostracized in the black community. Under these circumstances some black gay men may attempt to pass in black social settings as heterosexuals. Black gay men who rely exclusively on the black community for fulfilling their needs for play and love are likely to only partially validate their sexuality or same sex desires. Consequently, these men are less likely to enter a mature loving relationship with another man. Likewise, self-devaluation is likely to result when leisure contact in the black community requires the black gay to repudiate his homosexuality.

Other black gay men may seek to validate their sexuality without compromising their racial identity by fulfilling their needs for play and love through their involvement in the black community and the black gay community. Such an approach is less likely to result in discordance between one's sexual and racial identity. Subsequently, the individual's ability to effectively meet his needs for love and play as well as work are less likely to be jeopardized.

There is also a fourth alternative in seeking to fulfill the need for love and play. This alternative involves validating multiple identities by referring in selective ways to the black community, the gay community, and the black gay community. This mirrors the bicultural experience of all African Americans who must maneuver their lives between the predominantly white work setting and the predominately black social setting in which they love and play. Unlike heterosexuals, gay African Americans may sustain their psychosocial well-being through the selective use of three communities–the black, gay, and black gay communities. Consequently, it is important that human service workers be knowledgeable about the various alternatives available to black gays, and the possible effect that these involvements may have for his ability to positively address his needs for love, play and work as a gay African American.

AGE COHORT

The way black gay men attempt to achieve the developmental tasks of play, work, and love has a lot to do with their age. Age serves as a biological marker in that it is tied to physical growth (and decline) and cognitive development. It is also a social marker in that cultural and societal expectations impinge on people as a function of their age; youth are expected to attend school, adults are expected to work and raise families, and the elderly are expected to give themselves over to leisure activities.

In addition to biological and social markings, age is a historical marker. The attitudes and behaviors we form as a result of early life socialization will depend on the historical period in which we are born and raised. For instance, Herdt and Boxer (1993) direct our attention to four age cohorts among gays, each with its own separate experiences. The first cohort, elderly gays and lesbians, was raised under the norms prevailing between 1918 and 1940. These were years of intense and overt racial discrimination. Also, this was a period when objection to homosexuality was intense. The second cohort was raised during and after WW II, while the third was raised just after the Stonewall Riots and during the early years of gay activism. The members of this cohort were socialized largely during a time of growing efforts to end discrimination based on sexual orientation. The fourth cohort are those who were raised during the AIDS pandemic.

In applying the concept of age cohort to African American men, we will identify three broad age groups: adolescents (approximately 12 to 18 years of age), adults (20 to 59), and older adults (age 60 and older). Although the boundaries are broad and there may be individual differences, these three general age cohorts are helpful in understanding African American men.

Older Black Homosexual Men

Older African American homosexual men were raised in the period before WW II. Not only was homosexuality viewed as deviant behavior but white homosexuals, in spite of homosexuality itself being considered deviant, were likely to reject black homosexual men in love and play (Katz, 1976). This was also a time when gender role differences were important and relationships between men were caught up in the taking on of masculine and feminine identities and sexual practices.

Older gay African Americans were raised to view their sexual desires as a disease or a sin. These men are typically alienated from the modern gay community and are more likely to emphasize race as the primary component of their social identity. Few elderly black gay men associate openly with other gay black men. For many of them the idea that one could be black and gay at the same time is incomprehensible.

Adult Men

Adult black gays have grown up during a period of increased opportunities for African Americans resulting from the civil rights movement. This also includes an increase in opportunities to participate in mainstream homosexual institutions and organizations. This generation is increasingly integrating its sexual identity with its racial identity. The African American gay men who were surveyed in Bell and Weinberg's (1978) study are members of this age cohort. These men were likely to think of themselves as homosexuals and to deny that homosexuality was a sin or deviant. The integration of dual identities (sexual and racial) enables African American gay adults to be more vocal in articulating their concerns both to the gay and African American communities (Milloy, 1993; Poussaint, 1990). Their conscious attempt to integrate their racial and sexual identities has recently been propelled by the AIDS pandemic. African Americans are disproportionally affected by the disease, and the ineffectiveness of health services in both the gay and black communities has motivated them to speak out on their own behalf.

Adolescents

Young black gays are socialized in an era in which social attitudes on homosexuality have become more lenient and tolerant. These youth are seeing more on television and the media about positive gay lifestyles. Unlike earlier generations, they are also exposed to information through movies and documentaries such as *The Crying Game, Tongues Untied, Paris Is Burning,* and *Looking for Langston* that feature positive, or at least sympathetic, African American gay characters. Television programs that acknowledge homosexuality among African Americans are also relatively more common.

Black gay youth are demanding more positive black role models and evidence of inclusion in gay as well as black gay community organizations. They are growing up during a time in which despair and hopelessness seem to dominate the thoughts of many. The risk of AIDS and the threat of death from peer violence looms in their minds and can significantly affect their work, love and play choices.

GENDER BEHAVIOR AND MANNERISM

Researchers have shown that physical appearance is crucial to organizing the perceptions of others (Dion, Berscheid, & Walster, 1972; Strobe et al., 1971; Walster, Aronson, Abrahams, & Rottman, 1966). Moreover, the literature suggests that anti-gay prejudice and violence is often based on the degree to which an individual's behavior and physical appearance conform to social norms and cultural values on gender (Bohn, 1984; Cotton, 1992). The African American community continues to emphasize conformity to traditional male and female gender role appearance and expectations. As a result, for many men, acceptance by their African American peers requires a display of culturally prescribed male characteristics and mannerisms (Cunningham, 1993; Icard, 1986; Staples, 1982). Black youth whose physical characteristics and mannerisms are consonant with African American cultural gender definitions are likely to be affirmed by their peers. Conversely, black youth whose physical appearance is not consonant with African American male cultural expectations are likely to experience negative responses from their peers. This of course will especially be a problem when that youth also has homosexual inclinations.

The following account by Vernon (1983) illustrates how an African American youth's appearance and behavior negatively influenced how he was treated by his peers.

> I think I first realized I was a homosexual when people started calling me a faggot, and I really became aware of being a homosexual. . . . I think people started calling me faggot because of the way I acted, like I acted in sort of a way of always being with girls, and never playing around too much with the boys, and they began to associate that in some way with femininity, with being fem, and eventually, the word "sissy" arose, and I was classified. (p. 33)

Vernon (1983) goes on to describe his classroom experiences and how he responded to tirades of "faggot." He recounts how continual harassment by his male classmates finally resulted in a fight, which he won, but notes how defending himself resulted in sentencing to a juvenile correctional facility while his assailants went unpunished.

> When I walked out of the door, he was waiting behind the door and hit me in the face with a chain. I ran and they were chasing me, and they were catching up. All the time I was running I was reaching down in my drawers trying to pull out this razor, and eventually I got it out, and I just did a U-turn, and went blindly into them, cutting everybody who I could, and going after one person in particular who had hit me in the face with a chain. I cut his face up pretty bad, and I ran home . . . I came back to school the next day, and he was there with his mother, the police and everybody under the sun to take me to jail. (p. 36)

Of concern is whether helping professionals will respond to gender non-conforming youth in the punitive way that Vernon illustrates. If school, law and social service workers support traditional African American gender role norms, they can impose very negative psychosocial and developmental consequences on youth.

For adolescent and adult black men, African American gender expectations are closely linked with masculinity. Such expectations are associated with desires, stereotypical appearance and behavior such as virility, hypersexuality, toughness, and emotional aloofness (Majors & Billson, 1992; Staples, 1982). Men who do not conform to these prescriptions can be left with feelings of inferiority, gender confusion, and self-destructive behaviors.

On the other hand, effeminate behavior and mannerisms may also function as an adaptive defense mechanism in response to the stress from African American norms. Historically, European American transvestites and cross-dressers, two extreme types of "gender bending," have viewed themselves as sexually displaced people (Katz, 1976). Taking on a feminine appearance may enable African American gays to mock or reject black cultural expectations.

As feminine appearance and mannerism may or may not indicate developmental problems, helping professionals must be careful to assess psychosocial functioning independent of these physical attributes. Helping professionals need to identify the function of a feminine identity and how it is incorporated into the personality. The degree to which negative behavioral adaptations are incorporated into the personality is the determining factor, not appearance or mannerism.

SOCIOECONOMIC STATUS AND EDUCATION

Socioeconomic status, including level of education, is strongly related to the social and emotional problems experienced by minority group members (Ford & Norris, 1994; Kalichman, Kelly, Hunter, Murphy & Tyler, 1993). Socioeconomic status has also been shown to have an effect on the nature of sexual experiences among African Americans. Oggins, Veroff and Leber (1993) showed that lower income African Americans are more likely to engage in sex for pleasure than higher income African Americans.

Socioeconomic status appears to be related to the internalization of gender role stereotypes by African American men regardless of age cohort. Chauncey, Duberman and Vincinus (1989) point out that strict adherence to male and female roles in homosexual relations has been historically related to class. Additionally, Katz's

(1976) research on gay American history shows that in early homosexual gatherings the black homosexual male participants were primarily employed as chefs, chauffeurs, and domestics. Katz further notes that these black men frequently assumed a feminine role. More recently, the film, *Paris Is Burning* provides a glimpse into the African American, lower class, gay drag subculture. It depicts feminine gender identity of young, low income, black men. The young men depicted in this documentary have internalized idealized notions of traditional femininity. They join "houses" (collectives of men who idealize femininity, who form around a male who has a strong feminine identity and is placed in a prominent position), each with a name, and give over their lives to dressing outlandishly and competing in modeling contests.

Studies also suggest that socioeconomic status is related to friendship patterns among adult black gay men. Franklin (1992) observed that upwardly mobile African American men reported less commitment to their same sex friendships. He also noted that as adult gay African American men increase their participation in mainstream social institutions, their display of affection, intimate talks, and other characteristics of same sex friendship declines with other African American men. Franklin's observations are useful for understanding the friendship patterns among black gay men. Conceivably, the ability of upwardly mobile black gay men to effectively meet the developmental tasks of play and love may seriously be compromised by their isolation and alienation from other black gay men.

Interestingly, academic success may negatively affect friendship patterns among African American adolescents. African American youth may reject their academically successful peers as this suggests compliance with adult authority or with non-traditional male gender roles. In the documentary *Tongues Untied*, Marlin Riggs cogently describes the alienation he experienced as a result of his interest in academic achievement. He shows how peer rejection coupled with his desire for intimate (sexual) relations intensified his isolation and loneliness. These reports and observations suggest that helping professionals should explore how striving for economic and educational success may limit opportunities for friendship and intimate relations among adolescents, adult and older adult African American gays.

RELIGION

Unquestionably, the black church plays an important role in the lives of African Americans. Several studies point out the significance of the black church in the lives of black men (Parker & Smith, 1993; Taylor, 1988). Because of this a number of authors have called attention to the church's abhorrence of homosexuality and the belief that homosexuality is sinful (Butts, 1988; Mays et al., 1992; Peterson et al., 1992). To the extent that black gays have internalized negative religious beliefs, they are likely to experience dissonance between their spirituality and their sexuality. For example, Kenan's (1994) biography of James Baldwin illustrates how religion can negatively affect the life of an African American gay youth. Young Baldwin was raised in a family headed by an extremely religious stepfather. As a youth, Baldwin attended services both during the week and on Sunday and in addition he frequently preached sermons. Baldwin became extremely disturbed when he began to experience homosexual sexual desires. He referred to these feelings as the evil within. In his *Down at the Cross*, Baldwin wrote (Kenan, 1994):

> Owing to the way I had been raised, the abrupt discomfort that all this aroused in me and the fact that I had no idea what my voice or my mind or my body was likely to do next caused me to consider myself one of the most depraved people on earth. (p. 34)

Black gays who wish to participate actively in the black church may worry about public exposure of their sexuality or may be forced to decide between their spiritual and sexual fulfillment. Patterson (1983) who was active in Ebenezer Baptist Church (where Dr. Martin Luther King served as pastor), describes how he was forced to pretend he was heterosexual to advance in the church. He even feared that African American ministers, who themselves were gay and living double lives, would expose him to the congregation.

While the black church may have a negative impact on the lives of black gay men, the church may also serve a positive function as well. Patterson ironically recalls that church members tolerated his relationship with men as long as there was no obvious display of affection. He and his lover attended church gatherings together and even received mutual dinner invitations from members of the congregation. So long as black gays accept the need to mask their sexuality, negative church pressure may be offset by social, cultural and spiritual benefits. As observed by Parker and Smith (1993), the black church is especially important to the psychosocial well-being of older black gay men living in rural areas. Equally important, many of these men make significant contributions to their communities through service and leadership in the black church. Thus, the church serves as a major social and community outlet.

In examining the relationship between involvement in the black church and psychosocial functioning, social service workers must give careful consideration to the connection among spirituality, solidarity with the black community, and sexual identity. Just as appearance and mannerism may not indicate developmental problems, so too church involvement need not indicate an internalization of negative attitudes about homosexuality. Helping professionals need to examine how older men understand what they are doing and understand how they are balancing their social, spiritual, and sexual needs.

RURAL-URBAN DIFFERENCES

As the above discussion of the place of the black church in the lives of older rural gays suggests, urban-rural differences are an important area for assessment. Rural and urban differences are becoming less important as computer technology including bulletin boards, telephone services, and video and print media make it possible for African American gay men in rural areas to receive information about gay life that was once only available to men living in large cities. Nevertheless, attention to rural and urban distinctions may help in assessing sexual identity and psychosocial needs of black gays. As noted by Cass (1979), area of residence plays an important role in sexual development and in the formation of a gay sexual identity.

In general, African American adolescent males become involved in sexual behavior at an earlier age than white or Hispanic males (Kim, Marmor, Dubin, & Wolfe, 1993; Murray, 1992). Urban black youth become sexually active at an even earlier age than rural black youth (Alexander, Ensinger, Kim, Smith, Johnson, & Donald, 1989). Staples (1976) conjectures that unlike white middle class youth, the dating behavior of African American youth is by definition sexual behavior. Additionally, pressure to engage in sex is believed to be a rite of passage for many African American adolescent males (Icard, 1986).

Because African American adolescent norms stress involvement in heterosexual sex, gay adolescents will not find support for their sexual urges. The result is that they are likely to encounter peer pressure to engage in heterosexual sex, thereby confounding their ability to develop a healthy identity. In urban areas, the existence of gay-oriented organizations, self-help groups, bars and other organized meeting places mitigates the pressure toward heterosexuality and enables gay youth to find comfort and support.

Social services directed at gay minority youth are found in Chicago (Horizon House), New York (the Hetric-Martin Institute), Seattle (Lambert House), and other large cities. Similarly, urban and suburban gay white youth from upper-middle class families are becoming increasingly visible throughout the country and developing supportive relationships with their gay and bisexual peers (Gelman, Rosenberg, Quade, Roberts & Senna, 1993). This has influenced African American youth to also affirm their sexual orientation. The solace and support black gay youth sometimes receive from heterosexual African American female classmates (Duplechan, 1985) may facilitate this process.

In rural areas, however, the lack of organizations, self-help groups, bars and other gay institutions works against the development of a healthy sexual identity and behavior. Especially among lower income and relatively less educated persons, living in rural areas may serve to isolate African American gays regardless of their age. Coming out and finding supportive gay and heterosexual friends to associate, date and relax with are likely to be much more difficult accomplishments.

FAMILY AS A REFERENCE GROUP

Family life circumstances and dynamics are an important area for assessment, especially for adolescents living at home. In general, the family is the primary resource for meeting the psychosocial needs of African American youth. Careful consideration, however, is required lest a social worker assume that black families always serve a supportive role. For some youth, the African American family is a supportive network of personal relationships. For others, however, it is a collection of hostile and violent relationships. One major task for social service workers, then, will be to distinguish the supportive from the non-supportive.

Black gay youth, compared to Caucasian and Latino gay youth, report a higher incidence of gay-related assaults. Significantly, a large percentage of the violence occurs in their homes (Hunter, 1990). The extent to which a family maintains traditional, conservative expectations appears to be related to the likelihood that gay youth will experience negative family circumstances. Newman and Muzzonigro (1993) studied gay youth from traditional and non-traditional families. They defined traditional as those families that give high importance to religion, emphasize marriage and children, and do not speak English in the home. They found that minority youth from traditional families experienced less acceptance than those from non-traditional families. They also found that youth from traditional families were more likely to report feeling different from other boys and feeling stronger disapproval from family members.

The hostility that young African American gays experience at home may cause them to become estranged from their families. Taking this into account, it is not surprising that the families of the young men in the film *Paris Is Burning* were not shown. Although the director may not have intended to explore this issue, their absence suggests these young men were cut off and not receiving support from their families.

Family support is not just an issue for adolescents. As with black gay adolescents the relationship that adult black gay men have with their family may be characterized as supportive or non-supportive. In Bell and Weinberg's (1978) study black gay men were more likely than white gay men to perceive their family members as supportive. Notwithstanding these observations, other reports still describe the lack of support and acceptance that many black gay men experience both from the black community and their families because they are gay.

Increasingly, black families continue to involve African American men of all age cohorts. For instance, as men age they are expected to show involvement in the major decisions of family life. When a man doesn't marry, he may be expected to be available and to assist other family members as they attempt to meet their housing, economic and health needs. If the family does not recognize its need for gay friends and relationships, this can lead to major psychosocial problems. Adult and older adult African American gay men may often be caught between meeting their own and meeting the needs of other family members.

THE BLACK GAY COMMUNITY
AS A REFERENCE GROUP

Although family support remains important throughout the life course, adult and older adult African American gay men are more likely to find the support they need in their peer relationships. More than a decade ago Johnson (1982) identified two community sources available for normative information and psychosocial support–the African American community and the white gay community. This work suggests that gay African Americans must find their anchor in either the white gay community or in the heterosexual African American community. Today, however, there is a third choice: the African American gay community.

The African American gay community is not a new phenomenon. Graber (1989) reminds us that black gays and lesbians were a significant part of the Harlem Renaissance. While tolerated in the black community, Graber remarks that the social gatherings of black gays and lesbians in the 1920s and 1930s were often viewed by whites, both heterosexual and homosexual, as fashionably chic. The highly visible black gay and lesbian community of the roaring twenties disappeared with the advent of the Depression.

Sixty years later the vitality of a black gay and lesbian community has reemerged. Similar to the black gay and lesbian community of the 1920s, today's black gay community is a subculture that integrates aspects of the white gay and African American communities. As such it is evolving its own distinct language, sentiments and institutions. It is described in documentaries like *Tongues Untied* and the short stories appearing in *In the Life* (Beam, 1989) and *Brother to Brother* (Hemphill & Beam, 1991).

Tongues Untied, in particular, provides insights into the norms characterizing this emerging community. The documentary humorously describes "snapology," a way of expressing one's thoughts and feelings through accentuated snaps of the fingers combined with gyrated movements of the body. "Voguing," another distinct way of communicating described in the documentary, is a stylized form of dancing which mimics the behavior and mannerisms of female fashion models. "Voguing" was also highlighted in the documentary *Paris Is Burning*, suggesting that it is linked to lower socioeconomic sectors of the African American gay community.

Similar to the African American gay community of the 1920s, today's black gay community provides resources through which black gay men and lesbian women can have their social needs met. Unlike the black gay community of the 1920s, today's black gay community also provides the resources through which black gays and lesbians can address their health and mental health, as well as political and economic needs. A number of African American, gay-oriented self-help organizations have recently emerged and are becoming institutionalized. Many of these have surfaced through efforts to address the problem of AIDS. These organizations include "Gay Men of African Descent of New York City," the Washington-based "National Coalition of Black Lesbians and Gays," "The National Black Lesbian and Gay Leadership Forum," based in Los Angeles, and chapters of Brother-to-Brother, a social organization, which are forming throughout the country.

There is also the phenomenon of black gay churches that are emerging across the country. Additionally a number of magazines have emerged to address the needs of African American lesbian and gays such as *B & G: A Different Point of View*. Likewise, African

American gay writers, film makers, and openly black gay politicians, and scholars are all contributing to the sense of the new community forming among African American gays and lesbians. The emergence of these African American gay role models, self-help groups and organizations, offers resources that never existed before to adolescent, adult and older African American gays.

CONCLUSIONS

This article has outlined a multidimensional model for assessing the psychosocial well-being of African American gay men. The model gives special attention to the developmental tasks associated with work, play and love. These in turn are accomplished within the context of support and obstacles provided by family and community as reference groups, rural-urban living arrangements, and by the individual attributes of age, physical appearance, and socioeconomic status.

Although the dimensions of the model have been outlined, strategies for completing the assessment have not been presented. The model is long and requires time on the part of social service workers. However, the process should not be by-passed as it is a professional responsibility to view people in their unique circumstances, and to think about, order, and configure their case story toward the singular goal of appropriate and effective intervention (Meyer, 1993). The model also appears more linear than intended. As Meyer (1993) argues, too linear a process can limit data collection, which in turn limits our understanding of clients. Although we have only begun to suggest them, helping professionals should continue to explore the connections among the dimensions described here. For instance, we have suggested that age cohort needs to be taken into account with regard to all of the dimensions. Similarly, we have suggested that there are links between rural and urban issues, adolescent peer pressure, and socioeconomic status. We also suggest that helping professionals explore the possible effects of appearance, mannerisms, socioeconomic status, and education on the psychosocial well-being of black gay men.

REFERENCES

Alexander, C. S., Ensinger, M. E., Kim, Y. L., Smith, B. J., Johnson, K. E., & Doland, L. J. (1989). Early sexual activity among adolescents in small towns and rural areas: Race and gender patterns. *Family Planning Perspectives, 21*(6), 261-266.

Beam, J. (Ed.). (1989). *A black gay anthology: In the life.* Boston: Alyson.

Bell, A. P., & Weinberg, M. S. (1978). *Homosexualities: A study of diversity among men and women.* New York: Simon and Schuster.

Berger, R. M. (1982). The unseen minority: Older gays and lesbians. *Social Work, 27*(3), 236-242.

Berger, R. M. (1984). Realities of gay and lesbian aging. *Social Work, 29*(1), 57-62.

Berger, R. M., & Kelly, J. J. (1986). Working with homosexuals of the older population. *Social Casework, 67*(4), 203-210.

Bohn, T. R. (1984). Homophobic violence: Implications for social work practice. *Journal of Social Work & Human Sexuality, 2*(2-3), 91-112.

Butts, J. D. (1988). Sex therapy, intimacy, and the role of black population in the AIDS era. *Journal of the National Medical Association, 80,* 916-922.

Cass, V. C. (1979). Homosexual identity formation: A theoretical model. *Journal of Homosexuality, 4*(3), 219-235.

Chauncey, G., Jr., Duberman, M., & Vicinus, M. (1989). Introduction. In M. Duberman, M. Vicinus, & G. Chauncey, Jr. (Eds.), *Hidden from history: Reclaiming the gay & lesbian past* (pp. 1-13). New York: Meridan.

Chestang, L. W. (1980). Character development in a hostile environment. In M. Bloom (Ed.), *Life span development.* New York: MacMillan.

Clatterbaugh, K. (1990). *Contemporary perspectives on masculinity: Men, women, and politics in modern society.* San Franciso: Westview Press.

Cotton, P. (June 10, 1992). Attacks on homosexual persons may be increasing, but man 'bashings' still aren't reported to police. (Medical News & Perspectives). *The Journal of the American Medical Association, 267* (22), pp. 2999-3000.

Cunningham, M. (1993). Sex role influences of African American males: A literature review. *Journal of African American Male Studies, 1*(1), 30-37.

Dion, K. K., Berscheid, E., and Walster, E. (1972). What is beautiful is good. *Journal of Personality and Social Psychology, 24,* 285-90.

Duplechan, L. (1985). *Eight days a week.* Boston: Alyson.

Ford, K., & Norris, A. (1994). Urban minority youth: Alcohol and marijuana use and exposure to unprotected intercourse. *Journal of Acquired Immune Deficiency Syndromes, 7*(4), 389-396.

Franklin, C. W. (1992). Hey, Home-Yo, Bro: Friendship among black men. In P. M. Mardi (Ed.), *Men's friendships* (pp. 201-214). Newbury Park: Sage Publication.

Gary, L. E. (1978). Mental health: A conceptual overview. In L. E. Gary (Ed.), *Mental health: A challenge to the Black community.* Philadelphia, PA: Dorrance.

Gelman, D., Rosenberg, D., Quade, V., Roberts, E., & Senna, D. (1993, November 8). Tune in, come out. *Newsweek*. pp. 70,71.

Ginsberg, S. W. (1955). The mental health movement: Its theoretical assumptions. In R. Kotinsky & H. Witmer (Eds.), *Community programs for mental health*. Cambridge, Massachusetts; Harvard University Press.

Graber, E. (1989). A spectacle in color: The lesbian and gay subculture of jazz age Harlem. In M. Duberman, M. Vicinus, & G. Chauncey, Jr. (Eds.), *Hidden from history: Reclaiming the Gay & Lesbian past* (pp. 318-331). New York: Meridian.

Hemphill, E., & Beam, J. (Eds.). (1991). *Brother to brother*. Boston: Alyson.

Herdt, G., & Boxer, A. (1993). Birth of a culture: An Introduction. In G. Herdt & A. Boxer. *Children of horizon* (pp. 1-24). Boston, MA.

hooks, b. (1992). *Race looks: Race and representation*. Boston: South End Press.

Huizinga, J. (1955). *Homo ludens: A study of the play-element in culture*. New York: Beacon Press.

Hunter, J. (1990). Violence against lesbian and gay male youths. *Journal of Interpersonal Violence*, *5*(3), 295-300.

Icard, L. (1986). Black gay men and conflicting social identities: Sexual orientation versus racial identity. In J. Gripton & M. Valentich (Eds.), *Social work practice in sexual problems* (pp. 83-93). New York: The Haworth Press, Inc.

Icard, L., & Traunstein, D. (1987). Black, gay, alcoholic men: Their character and treatment. *Social Casework*, *68*, 267-272.

Icard, L., Schilling, R. F., El-Bassel, N. & Young, D. (1992). Preventing AIDS among Black Gay men and Black Gay and heterosexual male intravenous drug users. *Social Work*, *37*(5), 440-445.

Johnson, J. (1982). Influence of assimilation on the psychosocial adjustment of black homosexual men. *Dissertation Abstracts International*, *42*, 4620B.

Kalichman, S. C., Kelly, J. A., Hunter, T. L., Murphy, D. A., & Tyler, R. (1993). Culturally tailored HIV-AIDS risk-reduction messages targeted to African-American urban women: Impact on risk sensitization and risk reduction. *Journal of Consulting and Clinical Psychology*, *61*(2), 291-295.

Katz, J. (1976). *Gay American history: Lesbians and gay men in the U.S.A.* New York: Thomas Y. Crowell.

Kenan, R. (1994). *Lives of notable gay men and lesbians: James Baldwin*. New York: Chelsea House.

Kim, M. Y., Marmor, M., Dubin, N., & Wolfe, H. (1993). HIV risk-related sexual behaviors among heterosexuals in New York City: Associations with race, sex, and intravenous drug use. *AIDS*, 7, 409-414.

Kinsey, A. C., Pomeroy, W., & Martin, C. E. (1948). *Sexual behavior in the human male*. Philadelphia: W. B. Saunders & Co.

Loiacano, D. K. (1989). Gay identity issues among Black Americans: Racism, homophobia, and the need for validation. *Journal of Counseling & Development*, *68*, 21-25.

Majors, R., & Billson, J. M. (1992). *Cool Pose: The dilemmas of Black manhood in America*. New York: Lexington Books.

Mays, V. C., Cochran, S. D., Bellinger, G., Smith, R. G., Henley, N., Daniels, M., Tibbits, T., Victorriane, G. D., Osei, K. O., & Birt, D. K. (1992). The language of black gay men's sexual behavior: Implications for AIDS risk reduction. *The Journal of Sex Research, 29*(3), 425-434.

Meyer, C. (1993). *Assessment in social work practice.* New York: Columbia University Press.

Milloy, C. (1993, April 25). Black gays can spur black rights. *Washington Post.* p. B1.

Murray, S. O. (1992). Components of gay community in San Francisco. In G. Herdt (Ed.), *Gay culture in America: Essays from the field.* Boston: Beacon Press.

Newman, B. S., & Muzzonigro, P. G. (1993). The effects of traditional family values on the coming out process of gay male adolescents. *Adolescence, 28*(109), 213-226.

Oggins, J., Veroff, J., & Leber, D. (1993). Perceptions of marital interaction among black and white newlyweds. *Journal of Personality and Social Psychology, 65*(3), 494-511.

Oliver, W. (1989). African American males and social problems; Prevention through Afrocentric socialization. *Journal of Black Studies, 29*, 15-39.

Parker, K. D., & Smith, E. (1993). Religious participation among African American men: Demographic and familial differences. *Journal of African American Male Studies, 1*(1), 38-46.

Patterson, L. (1983). At Ebenezer Baptist Church. In M. J. Smith (Ed.), *Black men, White men.* San Francisco: Gay Sunshine Press.

Paul, W., Weinrich, J. D., Gonsiorek, J., & Hotvedt, M. (1982). *Homosexuality: Social, psychological, and biological issues.* Beverly Hills: Sage.

Peterson, J. L., Coates, T. J., Catania, J. A., Middleton, L., Hilliard, B., & Hearst, E. (1992). High-risk sexual behavior and condom use among gay and bisexual African American men. *American Journal of Public Health, 82*, 1490-1494.

Poussaint, A. F. (1990, September). An honest look at black gays and lesbians. *Ebony*, pp. 124, 126,130-131.

Staples, R. (1976). Introduction to Black sociology. New York: McGraw-Hill.

Staples, R. (1982). *Black masculinity: The black male's role in American society.* San Francisco: The Black Scholar Press.

Stewart, C. (1991, December). Double jeopardy. *The New Republic.* pp. 13-15.

Strobe, W., Insko, C. A., Thompson, V. D., & Layton, B. D. (1971). Effects of physical attractiveness, attitude similarity, and sex on various aspects of interpersonal attraction. *Journal of Personality and Social Psychology, 18*, 79-91.

Taylor, R. J. (1988). Structural determinants of religious participation among Black Americans. *Review of Religious Research, 30*, 114-125.

Vernon, R. (1983). Growing up in Chicago Black and Gay. In M. J. Smith (Ed.), *Black men, White men.* Gay Sunshine Press: San Francisco.

Walster, E., Aronson, V., Abrahams, D., & Rottman, L. (1966). Importance of physical attractiveness in dating behavior. *Journal of Personality and Social Psychology, 4*, 508-16.

Native American
Two-Spirit Men

Terry Tafoya
Douglas A. Wirth

SUMMARY. This paper reviews the historical and contemporary literature on sexual conduct and identity among Native American men. Sexual conduct between people of the same gender was institutionalized, that is, considered fully acceptable and normal, in many Native communities. In part, institutionalized same sex intimacy was supported by religious beliefs that acknowledged the existence of people (and gods) who were neither entirely male nor entirely female. Because of this, Native American men today are likely to reject such labels as homosexual, gay, or *berdache*, in favor of two-spirit men. Culturally sensitive ways of working with such Native American men are discussed. *[Article copies available from The Haworth Document Delivery Service: 1-800-342-9678. E-mail address: getinfo@haworth.com]*

It is also said that the two people created thus were *Altse hastiin* and *Altse asdzqq*. In the language of Bilagaana, the White Man, they would be called First Man and First Woman.

Terry Tafoya, PhD, is Executive Director, Tamanawit Unlimited, Suite 575, 1202 E. Pike Street, Seattle, WA 98122. Douglas A. Wirth, BA, is Public Policy Specialist, Coalition of Voluntary Mental Health Agencies, Inc., 120 West 57th Street, Suite 1014, New York, NY 10019.

[Haworth co-indexing entry note]: "Native American Two-Spirit Men." Tafoya, Terry and Douglas A. Wirth. Co-published simultaneously in *Journal of Gay & Lesbian Social Services* (The Haworth Press, Inc.) Vol. 5, No. 2/3, 1996, pp. 51-67; and: *Men of Color: A Context for Service to Homosexually Active Men* (ed: John F. Longres) The Haworth Press, Inc., 1996, pp. 51-67; and: *Men of Color: A Context for Service to Homosexually Active Men* (ed: John F. Longres) Harrington Park Press, an imprint of The Haworth Press, Inc., 1996, pp. 51-67. Single or multiple copies of this article are available from The Haworth Document Delivery Service [1-800-342-9678, 9:00 a.m. - 5:00 p.m. (EST). E-mail address: getinfo@haworth.com].

51

> . . . At the end of four days, *Altse asdzqq*, the First Woman, gave birth to twins. But they were neither entirely male nor entirely female. They were what the Navajo people call *nadleeh* . . . (Zolbrod 1984, p 51)
>
> *—From the Navajo Creation Story*

In the Navajo "gender war," where men and women separate from one another, the *Nadleeh* or sacred twins are so powerful they alone can bring about the reunification and continuation of the Human Race by reconciling the differences between First Man and First Woman (Zolbrod 1984:354). The *nadleeh* of the Navajo, their status and place in legend and history, are not unique in Native America.

NATIVE AMERICAN CONCEPTS OF GENDER

Of the over two hundred Native North American languages spoken today, at least two-thirds have terms, like *nadleeh*, that describe other genders beyond male or female (Roscoe, 1987). In the anthropological literature, these other genders are often subsumed under the term *berdache*, a corruption of a Mid-eastern term, dating from the Crusades, for someone who was a catamite, or male sex slave (Williams, 1985; Tafoya, 1992). The term *berdache* is increasingly falling out of favor with contemporary scholars, especially Native American ones. Paula Gunn Allen, noted writer and a Sioux/Laguna Lesbian, has written that the term *berdache* is misapplied when used to describe Native American lesbians and gay males. Since the *nadleeh* are not sex slaves, the term *berdache* has no relevance to American Indian men or women (Allen 1986, p 31). Because no term, however, has come to replace it, it will occasionally be used in this article.

Similarly, because of western linguistic and cultural limitations, Native terms such as *nadleeh*, or the Crow's *bote*, or the Lakota's *winkte* are reduced to terms like *berdache*, hermaphrodite, transvestite, or homosexual, none of which capture the idea of multiple genders. The idea of multiple genders challenges fundamental western assumptions of duality: either/or; right/wrong; good/evil; male/female; gay/straight. The western need to classify the world into binary categories is so powerful it becomes easier to force people into them or eliminate those that don't fit within them.

For example, in 1513, the Spanish "explorer" Balboa referred to these different Native biological men as "sodomites" and let loose his dogs to rip them apart and kill them (Goldberg 1992, p 180). This was the period of the Spanish Inquisition where it was normal to kill or maim individuals whose beliefs or practices were different from established Catholic orthodoxy. As a result, Native people soon learned not to openly discuss their ideas about sexuality and gender with outsiders.

In spite of such atrocities, historians like Williams (1986) have been able to describe "sexual diversity" among the Native peoples of the Americas. Early Spanish conquerors like Cortez wrote that Native mesoamerican men were ". . . all sodomites and practice that abominable vice" (Salmoral 1990, p 76). Nunez, reporting on the behaviors of Native men in the area we now call Florida, wrote: "And I saw a man married to another, and those are effeminate men, and impotent, who dress like women and do women's work and shoot arrows and are highly respected and among these we saw many effeminate men, as I say, and they are stronger than other men, and taller and can bear heavy loads" (Salmoral 1990, p 76).

A monograph on Peruvian figurine pottery described the following sexual subject matter in an examination of over one hundred pots:

31 percent illustrated heterosexual anal intercourse
24 percent the penis
14 percent oral intercourse
11 percent conventional heterosexual intercourse
6 percent zoophilia[1]
5 percent male masturbation
4 percent the vulva
3 percent homosexual anal intercourse
1 percent lesbianism
1 percent uncertain. (Tannahill, 1980, p 298)

---

1. Zoophilia means sex with an animal. From the point of view of Native peoples, however, such a depiction may more accurately have represented clan sex rather than sex with an animal, i.e., not sex with an actual deer but with someone from the deer clan.

It should be remembered that anal or oral intercourse even among married couples were sins punishable by death in Spain at the time Columbus set sail. This was in part due to the Spanish belief that a man's sperm contained a perfectly formed human being or homunculus (Cavendish, 1972, p 41). Accordingly, all life came from the father, with the mother contributing no more than a nest within the womb where the miniature person was inserted. Anal or oral intercourse was thought to prevent the sperm from entering the womb, thereby causing the death of the homunculus. This is also one reason why men were not supposed to masturbate. Spilling their seed upon the ground in the biblical fashion of Onan was believed to kill the homunculi and prevent the development of life in the womb. Having sex with another man was believed to double the number of "sperm people" wasted on the ground.

Diversity in sexual eroticism is more possible in cultures not constrained by such beliefs. This was very true for instance within Native North America where homosexual conduct involving a *nadleeh* was accepted and treated in a positive way (Williams, 1986). Not all agree, however, that this was the case. Gutierrez (1989), for instance, suggests the *berdache* (at least among the Pueblo people) was a "status degeneration." He argues that the *berdache* was not seen as an acceptable gender but rather was " . . . a social status a person was pressed into or assumed" (Gutierrez, 1989, p 65).

Although Gutierrez claims familiarity with Pueblo culture, he consistently judges them from a European perspective. For example, he describes an 1852 account where, at the request of the U.S. Surgeon General, "the Acoma's town chief brought" a *berdache* in for an examination by physicians. Gutierrez interprets this as an example of "status degeneration associated with these effeminates–[who] lost their social standing and family and were at the whim of any man who cared to use them" (Gutierrez, 1989, p 63).

In reality, Pueblo culture has accommodated European intrusion by the establishment of a "Governor" (a more accurate translation than "town chief") who was and still is, in the vast majority of the 19 remaining New Mexico Pueblos, responsible for secular interactions with non-Indians (Sando, 1992, p 14). Within Pueblo culture, it would have been unusual for a Governor not to have accompanied a *berdache*. By 1852, the United States had "annexed" what is now the state of New Mexico and there would have been no political possibility of refusing the Surgeon General's request. The result of the examination showed, as most other medical examinations of *berdache* have also shown, no physical abnormalities; there is no evidence to support the idea that *berdache* were actually hermaphrodites.

Gutierrez's work has been roundly criticized by Pueblo scholars such as Simon J. Ortiz. Ortiz, commenting on his *When Jesus Came, the Corn Mothers Went Away: Marriage, Sexuality, and Power in New Mexico, 1500-1846* wrote:

> Gutierrez's attitude, tone, and verbal style all reveal his personal glibness and disrespect, and this in no way endears him to the Pueblo people, especially the Acoma, about whom he writes in describing the 'dialogue' of Spanish invasion and Indian resistance. (Ortiz, in press)

Perhaps it is best to refer to Paula Gunn Allen's excellent analysis of a Keresan Pueblo cultural event work described from three points of view, that of a white male anthropologist, a feminist, and a Laguna-Acoma Pueblo person (Allen, 1986). This masterful treatment emphasizes how much one's own biases influence comprehension.

As Allen's analysis demonstrates, historical documents do not accurately recapture Native concepts of sexuality. These written records tell us more about Western cultural biases than those of Native culture. Native people were treated as "the enemy" and intense racial animosity overcame any attempt to be rational or objective. In such circumstances "those one opposes are automatically called perverted" (Tannahill, 1980, p 168). Thus, the Spanish accusation "all these men are sodomites" was used to justify their conquest much in the manner of contemporary anti-gay efforts by Christian extremists.

In the majority of contemporary Native communities, the combined influence of forced attendance in federal boarding schools, Christian missionaries, and continual intrusion of European/American culture, has had such an impact that the role of the *berdache* in most reservations has been permanently altered, if not eliminated. We believe six levels of gender may be tracked among Native

Americans today: a hyper-masculine male (males raised as warriors away from females), a "standard" male, a *berdache*, a biological female *berdache* (sometimes referred to as an "Amazon"), a "standard" female, and a hyper-feminine female.

The Gay, Lesbian, and Bisexual (Lesbigay) movement, and the growing acceptance of transgenderism within the transsexual community, have resulted in many younger Native people referring to themselves as Gay, Lesbian, Bisexual, Transgendered, or Transsexual, rather than as a *berdache*, or the tribal equivalent of a *berdache*. This likely reflects the health of a living culture: only dead or stagnant cultures remain the same. In addition, since the late 1980s, the quest for empowerment and self-definition has lead to an annual gathering of Native Lesbigays and their friends and supporters held alternately in the United States and Canada. This group has sanctioned the use of the term "Two-Spirit" as a way of acknowledging specific Native terms, such as *nadleeh*, while moving away from the non-Native anthropological term *berdache*, and what many believe are the European-American categories of Gay, Lesbian, Bisexual, or Transgendered.

The tribal concept of Two-Spirit describes an individual who has both a male and female spirit. As discussed earlier, it is believed that the Two-Spirit person had a place of respect in many tribes: if one is a woman, one sees the world as a woman; if one is a man, one sees the world as a man, but to be Two-Spirit means one can see in both directions, and therefore understand the world in a more holistic manner.

In reality, it is likely that attitudes about the Two-Spirit varied widely among Native American cultures: some exalted them, some were indifferent, and some were openly hostile. It is also possible, from a Native point of view, that one's *berdache* status was less important than one's overall personality and behavior. In other words, a "good and valuable person" was respected independently of gender role (Tafoya and Rowell, 1988). For native people, the difficulty with the concepts lesbian, bisexual or gay is that the *berdache* was not seen as a sexual orientation but as gender role (not entirely male or female) with a strong spiritual component. Since there is no spiritual/religious component to being Lesbigay, gayness doesn't capture the idea of *nadleeh, bote, winkte* or other

Native terms. In this regard it is useful to picture the notion of Lesbigay and Native terms as a Venn diagram–two circles that overlap somewhat in content but that do not completely cover one another.

Native Americans prefer to understand things in terms of circles rather than categories like either/or. The circle is comprised of an infinite number of points. Thus, the Native American gender circle is one with limitless points that change over time and across contexts.

HISTORICAL BACKGROUND

There is no guarantee that Native American clients will understand gender in the traditional ways being described here. As a result of oppressive circumstances, many Native clients have lost the connection with their heritage. Native Americans differ from other American ethnic groups because of Treaty Rights–formal and binding contracts signed between the Federal government and American Indian Nations. For example, as a result of contracts, eligible American Indian and Alaskan Native people have access to services through the Indian Health Services, the Bureau of Indian Affairs, and Indian Education programs.

Tragically, these same contracts made Indian communities "wards" of the government with little self-determination. Prior to the Indian Child Welfare Act of 1978, it was estimated that twenty-five percent of all Native American children were reared away from Native homes, either adopted or put in foster care with white Americans. Since then the situation has changed somewhat but it is still likely that many Native adult clients will have had such an experience. They will be part of the "lost" children, with little knowledge of the tribal tradition.

In the 1950s, the federal government initiated two policies that led to increased isolation of tribal traditions. Under the policy of relocation, Native people were encouraged (with one-way tickets paid for by the federal government) to leave their reservations and "relocate" in major urban areas, such as New York, Chicago, or Los Angeles. This had the effect of limiting their access to the resources available to those living on or near their reservation.

Because of this policy, 60% of Native American people now live in urban areas. Under the policy of termination, tribal status was actually "terminated"–rather like passing a federal law that African-Americans would no longer be officially recognized as a people. Both of these policies were designed to minimize or eliminate federal treaty obligations. These terrible policies have had an untold and devastating impact on Native American culture, psychosocial health, and family dynamics.

There is also an historic "jurisdictional dispute" which has worsened during times of federal and state budget cuts. Native people become caught between state agencies who want them to seek federal (treaty-based) services and federal agencies who want them to seek state (non-treaty based) services. This dispute leads to the denial of service. In the same manner, some Native people are so accustomed to receiving federal services, they may be unaware of state, city, and private programs. American Indians have only been citizens of the United States since 1924. Some states have a history of open hostility toward reservations since their laws often did not apply on the (federal-reserved land) reservation and thus they lost revenues that otherwise would have been theirs. For example, just as one does not pay state sales tax in a military-based PX, one can obtain alcohol and cigarettes at a lower cost from reservation stores that sell such goods. The advent of gambling casinos on reservations (where states cannot regulate) has increased the tension between many states and Native American Nations.

Boarding and missionary schools (often the same thing) were major sources of physical and sexual abuse for Native boys and girls. The extent and severity of sexual abuse is only recently being acknowledged. Out of the 350 male participants at a Canadian Native workshop held in the early 1990s, fewer than ten had not experienced some form of sexual abuse (Tafoya, in press). Some individual Native people may have difficulty reconciling their sexual orientation with their sexual abuse. They may feel degraded and defective and attribute their sexual identity to "what was done to me." While such feelings are not unusual for any Lesbigay person with a similar history, the frightening frequency of sexual abuse among Native people makes it a significant issue to consider therapeutically.

Since family members have been going to boarding school for generations, some Native people have no memory of how to be a parent. As mentioned, boarding schools had an overwhelmingly negative impact on maintaining the integrity of traditional concepts of gender and sexuality. During adolescence, instead of receiving instruction on their traditions, they were socialized into western sexual ideas and practices. As a result, many Native people have had as little informed instruction about Native sexuality and gender as most other Americans.

There is sometimes a semantic difficulty with the term "boarding school," which often conjures up ideas of upper-class educational institutions in Switzerland. Federal Boarding Schools were established for Native American children for the purpose of eradicating Native culture and language, with forced removal of children from their homes, often by the age of five. This was for the express purpose of "civilizing the savages." At boarding school, children were beaten for speaking their own language and were often kept away from their parents for years at a time. Native American students were not officially permitted to attend public schools until the 1930s.

Some clients will also have experienced identity confusion because of having been raised in non-Native homes. Prior to the passage of the Indian Child Welfare Act, research showed such young people had rates of attempted suicide that were up to five times higher than their peers (Tafoya, 1990). This is another potential "danger zone" clinicians may want to consider in screening interviews. Conflict seems to arise when one's self-identity (psychologically identifying with the adoptive, non-Native parents) and the perceived identity (recognized as a "non-white" in a racist society) do not integrate. One can then see that the addition of a Gay or Lesbian identity can further complicate matters.

As with members of other ethnic groups, not all Native individuals who engage in homosexual behavior will self-identify as Gay or Lesbian, which they may consider a "white" way of thinking about the self. In European-American culture, one's identity is often performance-based: one is what one does, a professional or a homosexual, for example. For many Native people, the core identity is what one is (one's tribe or family–an identity that will never alter).

For some tribal men, one's identity as a homosexual may not be defined by the gender of one's partner, but by the nature of the act itself; thus, as long as one is the active insertor, the gender of one's partner is irrelevant. The only "homosexual" involved is the man who passively receives. Such ideas are normative in a number of Native communities, and must be understood from that context.

For those Native individuals who come from this cultural standpoint, the social service worker should not assume the person is denying his sexual orientation. Rather, the worker should explore how the person understands his or her sexuality. For those gay, lesbian, or bisexual therapists who have spent a great deal of effort coming to terms with their own sexual orientation, there may be an inappropriate tendency to project their own struggle on to their Native client.

For many Native Americans, there is a strong emphasis on the family, and some may be concerned with meeting family obligations, especially with regard to becoming a parent. In some Native communities, a person is not considered an adult until one has fathered or raised a child. This is less of a concern with Native lesbians, who may have biological children of their own.

In research on inter-racial same-sex couples, there was a higher rate of heterosexual experience reported among Native Americans than with any other ethnic group. This high incidence of functional bisexuality may reflect the more fluid role of the traditional *berdache* (Tafoya & Rowell 1988). A mental health professional might remind a childless Native gay man of the tradition within many tribes of assuming an active parent type role, fostering children, or becoming a more involved uncle to nephews and nieces. Indeed, in some tribes, the oldest maternal uncle served as a child's primary disciplinarian. In other words, not having a biological child of one's own is not a reason for a Native male to lose the opportunity to be a parent.

In many traditional cultures, a child would become the "social security" of an elder, so someone without children would "acquire" a child through formal or informal adoption. Because of the severe disruption of traditional family roles due to the interference of the federal government, many Native men would benefit from exploring various contemporary models of appropriate and effective parenting.

Like many Lesbigays, the incidence of substance abuse among Native people is high. Our observations of the effects of oppressive circumstances lead us to argue that Native people are very vulnerable to substance abuse and endure high rates of Post-Traumatic Stress Disorder (PTSD).

Although reliable and valid data are unavailable, cross-cultural studies of depression suggest that Native Americans, including Alaska Natives, are often diagnosed and treated for clinical depression (Shore & Manson, 1981). Furthermore, we suggest that clinically depressed Native Americans are likely to self-medicate with alcohol and other drugs. Because the underlying depression is not diagnosed, the client is led into an unending cycle of substance use and abuse. There is some evidence that the onset and duration of depression in Native Americans is manifested differently than in whites, which may interfere with diagnosis (Tafoya 1990).

IMPLICATION FOR PRACTICE

This paper will not cover specific and concrete issues related to effectively working with Native people, gay or otherwise. Nevertheless, in the following section we will address some skills that should prove useful for mental health professions.

One practice issue that is worth noting has to do with language. William Leap (personal communication) shows the influence of a second language across three generations. He distinguishes between native speakers of English and those who use English. Most Native Americans are best thought of as English users. In other words, if one's grandparents or parents spoke a language other than English, then one will not tend to process English in the manner of a native speaker of English, even if English is the only language available for communication. It then becomes easy to misdiagnose some language-based communication problems as resistance or hostility. For example, all languages have a "pausetime," an interval that signals when someone has finished and when someone else may speak. For native speakers of English, this pausetime will last an average of one second. For a number of Native languages, the pausetime may be significantly longer than one second. In a group setting, those clients with the shortest pausetime will automatically dominate discussions, while those with the longest pausetimes may never have an opportunity to speak.

There are a range of skills involved in working effectively with Native American clients including: developing alliances with clients; gathering of culturally relevant information; discussing culturally sensitive issues and negotiating culturally-appropriate interventions. When the mental health worker lacks these skills, service can become less than adequate, if not harmful.

Native men in crisis from the stress of problems and disease often fall back on culturally defined modes of coping with difficulties. These ways of coping with stress, frustration and discrimination can be recognized by the C.A.R.E. model.[2]

C onfrontation (Aggression/Defensiveness)
A ccommodation ("Yes" is better than "No")
R etreat (Avoidance/Withdrawal)
E mpowerment (Separatism/Creativity) (Tafoya, 1992)

Mental health professionals would do well to note that these same strategies will often occur on the individual as well as on the organizational level. The C.A.R.E. model describes coping strategies. People will often shift back and forth among them depending on cultural influences, the amount of stress being experienced, and the power differences among those in the crisis situation.

Confrontation is often used when feelings of powerlessness combine with a moral or ethical conviction that an agency or individual should be responding in a certain way, but is not ("You're not providing me the medication I should have . . . let me talk to your supervisor!"). Incidentally, some researchers suggest that behavioral/cultural differences will be misinterpreted by therapists as confrontational.

---

2. The C.A.R.E. and T.I.P.S. models discussed here were created by the authors and appeared in curriculum packages designed for the American Psychological Association's National AIDS Training Project, and in the National Series of HIV Frontline Forums 1992.

Accommodation is frequently used when there is a perceived power difference coupled with a lack of expectation that the mental health worker will alter his/her behavior in response to a request or a confrontation. The statement "Yes" is better than "no" relates to an old joke taught to young American Indians in the southwest: if they say "Yes," when a non-Indian asks a question, then the non-Indian will stop asking questions, but if they say "no," then the non-Indian will ask more questions. Accommodation is often the surface acceptance of something, but not the actual acceptance.

Retreat is characterized by the avoidance or withdrawal from the interaction or from potential interaction. In Native American country, the saying "voting with one's feet," means to walk out of a meeting without saying anything as a statement of disapproval. This may lead to problems when European Americans assume that silence means consent. In many cases Native Americans do not use agencies or services because they don't want to endorse or support them. Depending on the overall level of stress, a Native client might interact with an insensitive clinician or organization one time but feel too taxed to do so another. As noted in Anderson, Landry and Kirby (1991, p 117):

> . . . we must appreciate that minorities, because of their long-standing history of having suffered discrimination and oppression, do not always perceive institutions and governmental agencies as supportive, but may instead consider them intrusive and view them with mistrust and suspicion . . . This mistrust is often mistakenly viewed as a lack of concern . . .

Empowerment often occurs when a conventional service fails to meet basic needs, leading people to look for new ways of doing things. Sometimes this leads to separatism or the establishment of new services. This was the case with regard to the establishment of services for AIDS/HIV such as the Gay Men's Health Crisis in New York City, the People of Color Against AIDS Network in Seattle, the National Native American AIDS Prevention Center, the Gay Asian Pacific Alliance's HIV Project, the National AIDS Task Force for the Association of Black and White Men Together, all in the Bay area of California. Each organization has a specific focus aimed at meeting the needs of specific communities.

Service providers should also be aware of the "flip side" of ethnic specific concerns. Even though there may be specific Native American programs available within a given area, a Native client may deliberately choose a mainstream service to insure confidentiality, especially if the difficulties being experienced include sexual issues.

Culture enables "a people," Native or Lesbigay, to survive the hostile larger environment. Culture represents the accumulated wisdom of "a people," including Lesbigay people. Change or adaptation (internal or externally forced in the face of attempted cultural obliteration) occurs over time and requires the use of all available cultural resources. Here the parallel between Native Americans and the Lesbigay community should be painfully clear. As members of the dominant culture, European-Americans generally assume cultural superiority (implicitly or explicitly). Although Native American clients may be "OK," European-Americans often act as if they know the one right or true way. In the same manner, heterosexist mental health professionals often put down the Lesbigay client. In addition, European-Americans generally believe mental health professionals use methods that are "value free," objectively verifiable, and self-evident (Stewart, 1989, p 91). However, it is clear that America has an unfortunate history of racism, a system of oppression for a social purpose. Racism is sustained by both personal attitudes and structural forces, even those of a supposedly therapeutic nature.

Gay, bisexual, or Two-Spirit men face overlapping forms of cultural struggle and oppression: a dominant/straight society's racism, sexism, and homophobia. They also confront racism and sexism within the Lesbigay community itself: Native Americans are not always accepted as friends and lovers, exercise little control in decisionmaking, and generally do not participate in the leadership structure of the gay movement. They also are likely to be involved in a struggle over an independent cultural identity that encompasses many levels of personal understanding (spiritual, mental, emotional, and physical). To assume the priority of any component of an identity (ethnic, gender, etc.) without verifying this with a client can represent a form of professional malpractice.

As a way of "taking back" or reclaiming power, many Lesbigay people have entered the mental health field. However, as providers who are strongly committed to a Lesbigay identity, they must be cautioned not to impose this on Native clients. This is why "Lesbigay" or transgendered is used in this article, even though the focus of this paper is on gay men of color. Some Native "male" clients may not identify as "Gay" or, indeed, as "men." In other words, part of the effort to respect a client is to allow the client to express his (or whatever personal pronoun a client identifies with) central identity. The mental health worker may mistakenly see a client as Native-American by appearance alone without bothering to consider who his parents were or whether he grew up on a reservation.

Even when a Native American identifies "gayness" as a critical component of his identity, the mental health worker should be cautioned against automatically using standard Lesbigay resources as part of an intervention. It is important to remember the "Gay community" has not been the community of hope, love, and acceptance for many people of color as it has been for many Gay White men. The issue of AIDS/HIV, the early struggle over the limitations of funding and other resources, changing epidemic demographics and needs, continue to polarize the Lesbigay community in a manner that negatively affects Native Americans. Attempting to provide the most appropriate services to diverse populations, especially Two-Spirit Native Americans, is perhaps best seen as an on-going process, rather than a final accomplishment.

Mental health professionals are offered these final "TIPS" or guidelines for multiculturally competent practice with Native American clients:

T echnique effectiveness will not be total so long as only one approach, one intervention or one curriculum is used.

I ntegration and assimilation are not the goals of all Native people; willingness to integrate and assimilate will vary according to an individual perceived stress and level of power.

P articipation will vary according to the Hierarchy of Needs (Maslow, 1968). Someone in need of safety and survival will not pay attention to information directed at the need for self-actualization.

S ponsorship = Ownership. It is critical to involve Native American client groups in the planning phases of service planning and treatment. If someone is made to feel like a "rubber stamp," approving decisions already made by administrators, they will reject action plans and programs.

We would like to conclude by outlining the pitfalls that need to be avoided in order to become culturally competent.

1. Lack of understanding of culture and its relative influence on the client system.
2. Retention of stereotyped images.
3. Use of standard techniques and approaches exclusively–the idea there is only "ONE RIGHT WAY!"
4. Failure to understand and acknowledge power issues.
5. Assuming a mutuality of interest between client and professional helper.
6. Failure to see the inter-relationships of the multiple identities of clients.

REFERENCES

Allen, P. G. (1986). *Mending the sacred hoop: The refeminization of American Indian literature*. Boston, MA: Beacon Press.

Anderson, J. R., C. P. Landry, & J. Kirby (Eds.). (1991). *AIDS: Abstracts of the psychological and behavioral literature*. Washington DC.: American Psychological Association.

Cavendish, M. (Ed.). (1992). *Encyclopedia of love and sex* (p. 41). New York: Crescent.

Goldberg, J. (1992). *Sodometries*. Palo Alto, CA: Stanford University Press.

Gutierrez, R. (1989). Must we deracinate Indians to find gay roots? *Outlook, 2*(3), 61-67.

Gutierrez, R. (1991). *When Jesus came the corn mothers left: Marriage, family and power in New Mexico, 1500-1846*. Palo Alto, CA: Stanford University Press.

Maslow, A. H., Synergy in the society and in the individual. *Journal of individual psychology, 20*, 153-64.

Ortiz, S. J. (in press). Commentary on, "When Jesus came the corn mothers left: Marriage, family and power in New Mexico, 1500-1846." *Journal of American Indian Culture and Research*.

Roscoe, W. (1987). Bibliography of *berdache* and alternative gender roles among North American Indians. *Journal of Homosexuality, 14*(3/4), 81-171.

Salmoral, M. (1990). *America 1492: Portrait of a continent 500 years ago.* NY, NY: Facts on File.

Sando, J. (1992). *Pueblo nations: Eight centuries of Pueblo Indian history.* Santa Fe, NM: Clear Light Publishers.

Shore, J. H., & S. M. Manson. (1980). Cross-cultural studies of depression among American Indians and Alaska Natives. *White Cloud Journal, 2*(2), 5-12.

Stewart, T. (1989). *HIV prevention curriculum. National Association of Black and White Men Together.* San Francisco, CA.

Tafoya, T. (1990). Circles and cedar: Native Americans and family therapy. In G. Sava, B. Karrer, & K. Hardy (Eds.), *Minorities and family therapy* (pp. 71-98). Binghamton, NY: The Haworth Press, Inc.

Tafoya, T. (1992). Two-spirit: Native lesbians and gays. In B. Berzon (Ed.), *Positively gay: New approaches to gay and lesbian life* (pp. 57-62). Berkeley, CA: Celestial Arts.

Tafoya, T. (in press). Epistemology of Native American healing and family psychology. *Journal of Family Psychology.*

Tafoya, T., & Rowell, R. (1988). Counseling gay and lesbian Native Americans. In M. Shernoff & W.A. Scott (Eds.), *Sourcebook on lesbian/gay health care* (pp. 63-67). Washington, DC.: National Lesbian and Gay Health Foundation.

Tanahill, R. (1980). *Sex in history.* New York: Stein & Day.

Williams, W. (1985). Persistence and change in the *berdache* tradition among contemporary Lakota Indians. *Journal of Homosexuality, 11*(3/4), 191-200.

Williams, W. (1986). *Spirit and the flesh.* Boston: Beacon Press.

Zolbrod, P.G. (1984). *Dine bahane: The Navajo creation story.* Albuquerque, NM: University of New Mexico Press.

Homosexually Active Latino Men: Issues for Social Work Practice

Carlos E. Zamora-Hernández
Davis G. Patterson

SUMMARY. This paper presents a critical overview of the literature on homosexual conduct and identity among Latino men both in Latin America and in the United States. The relationships between homosexually active Latino men and their families, the various Latino national origin communities, and gay communities are also considered. Latino perspectives are contrasted with the dominant North American gay understandings of homosexuality in terms of individual identity and political activism. The unique problems of this population are also discussed with an emphasis on the social and cultural resources available to homosexually active Latinos and social work practitioners who serve them. Recommendations for social work practice and further research are offered. *[Article copies available from The Haworth Document Delivery Service: 1-800-342-9678. E-mail address: getinfo@haworth.com]*

INTRODUCTION

Providing effective services to homosexually active Latinos challenges us to understand the nature of minority identities and com-

Carlos E. Zamora-Hernández, MSW, is affiliated with University of Washington, School of Social Work, 4101 15th Avenue NE, Seattle, WA 98195. Davis G. Patterson, MA, is affiliated with University of Washington, Department of Sociology, 202 Savery Hall, Seattle, WA 98195.

[Haworth co-indexing entry note]: "Homosexually Active Latino Men: Issues for Social Work Practice." Zamora-Hernández, Carlos E. and Davis G. Patterson. Co-published simultaneously in *Journal of Gay & Lesbian Social Services* (The Haworth Press, Inc.) Vol. 5, No. 2/3, 1996, pp. 69-91; and: *Men of Color: A Context for Service to Homosexually Active Men* (ed: John F. Longres) The Haworth Press, Inc., 1996, pp. 69-91; and: *Men of Color: A Context for Service to Homosexually Active Men* (ed: John F. Longres) Harrington Park Press, an imprint of The Haworth Press, Inc., 1996, pp. 69-91. Single or multiple copies of this article are available from The Haworth Document Delivery Service [1-800-342-9678, 9:00 a.m. - 5:00 p.m. (EST). E-mail address: getinfo@haworth.com].

munities. To do this, we present a critical overview of the literature on Latino men, keeping in mind that this population has been unevenly studied with selective attention to AIDS at the expense of other areas. We consider homosexual conduct and identity first in Latin America and then among Latinos in the United States. This backdrop sets the stage for an analysis of Latinos in the varied milieux where questions of identity and community become salient: family, the different Latino national origin communities, and gay communities, including important differences within and across these groupings. Throughout, our focus is not only on social problems, but also on the social and cultural resources available to gay Latinos and social work practitioners who serve them.

The central themes of identity and community require a word about nomenclature. Although we include all persons of Latino or Hispanic descent, there is no all-inclusive, politically neutral term to describe them (de la Garza, Falcon, Garcia, & Garcia, 1992). The Latino population is composed of many groups which consider themselves culturally distinct. We include men from all Spanish or Portuguese speaking nations of the Americas. In addition to thinking of themselves as culturally distinct, Latinos consider race to be a continuous rather than fixed set of categories. In terms of race, the three main groups are Euro-African Latinos, Euro-Indigenous-Latinos and European-Latinos, but usually self-reference is based on national origin rather than racial characteristics. These facts of ethnic and racial identity create problems of communication and understanding between Latinos and non-Latinos and even among Latinos themselves, all of which are important to the study of sexual conduct and identity.

Likewise, to understand homosexuality among Latino men is to appreciate variety. Just as all Latinos are not alike, neither are Latino men who engage in homosexual behavior all alike. What men who have sex with men should be called raises difficult sociopolitical questions even in the United States (d'Emilio, 1983). Using the term "gay," therefore, to define all or most Latino men who have sex with other men is a serious problem. Furthermore, the concepts of gay and gay culture as understood in the United States are somewhat foreign to Latin American nations, even among some Latinos who label themselves gay or homosexual (Arguelles &

Rich, 1989; Lancaster, 1986, 1988; Murray & Arboleda, 1987). Because of these difficulties we will use the terms homosexually active or involved and men who have sex with men. We will also distinguish homosexual conduct—the act of having sex with another man—from homosexual identity—the belief that one is a homosexual.

The problem of what to call oneself is more than just academic: it creates a dilemma for Latino men in the United States because it pits family identity against sexual identity, ethnic community against the gay community. Gay men who belong to ethnic minority groups are usually faced with a conflict between their sexual identity and the ethnic identity of their family of origin (Icard, 1986; Morales, 1990). The conflict leads some to think of themselves as Latino gays, others as gay Latinos, and still others as neither. How the conflict is resolved depends on personal values operating within the constraints posed by one's social environment.

While recognizing the danger of glossing over these and other important distinctions by talking of Latino men as a group, the scant research in this area constrains us. We bring together perspectives from varied sources, but they only manage to capture some of the diversity and complexity of experience among Latino men who have sex with men. For this reason, our discussion of Latin America should not be viewed as a monolithic conception of Latino homosexuality everywhere at all times, but as useful cultural background to the situations of diverse Latinos in the U.S.

HOMOSEXUAL CONDUCT AND IDENTITY IN LATIN AMERICA

Although Latin American nations are culturally distinct, norms of homosexual conduct and identity appear to cut across them. Studies of homosexuality in locations as diverse as Argentina, Brazil, Costa Rica, Cuba, Mexico, Nicaragua, and Peru point to a similar set of norms. The reader should keep in mind, however, that the international gay liberation movement is affecting Latin America, creating differences that depend on processes of modernization taking place within countries and the level of integration into the international community.

A survey of the legal systems of Latin American nations would show that although homosexuality is legal in most countries, the police sometimes use public morality laws to harass homosexuals, particularly those of the lower classes and those who are more flamboyant (Arboleda, 1987; Tielman & Hammelburg, 1993). Persecution and murder of known homosexuals are not uncommon in some countries, such as Brazil and Mexico (Mott, 1990; Murray & Taylor, 1990). But two factors combine to create circumstances in which homosexual activity may be less taboo than in the U.S.: a legal tradition of "overt indifference" that minimizes interference with individuals' private lives (Arguelles & Rich, 1989; Murray & Taylor, 1990; Taylor, 1986), and a system of gender and sexual ideology that presents opportunities for homosexual activity with little threat to a man's heterosexual, masculine identity (Arboleda, 1987; Lancaster, 1988; Murray, 1987a; 1990).

Machista[1] Homosexuality

In general, Latin American homosexual conduct is based on gender-role differentiation (Gilmore & Uhl, 1987). Anal intercourse is emphasized, and individuals show a propensity to play either the receptive or insertive sexual role–analogous to traditional heterosexual passive-feminine and active-masculine roles (Carrier, 1976a; Lancaster, 1988; Magaña & Carrier, 1991). Homosexual identity, both in terms of one's own perceptions of oneself and labeling by others, refers in this context almost exclusively to the person assuming the receptive-passive role. The active participant does not usually consider himself homosexual, and in fact, his own sense of masculinity may even be boosted (Arboleda, 1987; Murray, 1990).

Lancaster (1988) notes that in Nicaragua, it is not unknown for an *activo* to brag of his homosexual exploits among his male heterosexual friends, boosting his own and even others' sense of his masculinity. Thus the determination of homosexual identity is

---

1. The word *machista* derives from *machismo*, the Latin American system of gender roles and ideology that assigns men the tasks of providing for family members' economic security, physical safety, and protection of their good name. This system also requires men to be dominant, aggressive, and hyper-masculine, whereas women are expected to be morally superior and submissive.

based largely on the role taken in the sex act. In contrast, North American identity norms are based largely on the object of arousal such that any same-sex conduct threatens one's heterosexual, masculine identity. Furthermore, even though playing the *passive* role is certainly stigmatized, by virtue of their inclusion in the sexual practices of "ordinary men," Lancaster argues that *pasivos* are still less marginalized than North American gays (Lancaster, 1988, p. 114).

However, Murray (1990) cautions that these ideal categories can be slippery. *Pasivos* may not think of themselves as gay or homosexual, and even masculine men who play the passive role on occasion may not feel their masculinity threatened.

To further complicate the issue of identity, many Latino men who have sex with men also sustain sexual relations with women (Carrier, 1989). Studies of HIV transmission in the U.S. confirm that Latino men show significantly higher rates of bisexuality than whites (Chu, Peterman, Doll, Buehler, & Curran, 1992; Diaz et al., 1993). In a study of seropositive blood donors, 34% of the Latino subjects reporting sex with men identified themselves as heterosexuals, clearly showing the differences in sexual identity norms for Latinos and non-Latinos (Doll, Petersen, White, Johnson, & Ward, 1992). Furthermore, few of the subjects indicating heterosexual or bisexual orientation reported ties with the gay community, indicating an absence of gay consciousness or identity.

These general norms can be explained in part by the tendency of Latin American men to isolate their homosexual behavior from other roles and activities, such as father or husband. Because homosexual activity is thought to be inconsistent with these other valued roles, compartmentalization of homosexuality prevents cognitive dissonance over competing and inconsistent roles (Murray, 1987, 1990).

In his research on Mexico, Carrier (1989) notes that when homosexual activity does lead to internal conflicts, the dissonance is typically greatest for masculine men who play an active role, perhaps because their activities with men can cause them or others to question their own sexual identities. These observations indicate that desire for other men carries at least some implications for one's sexual identity, even if the role one plays is the most important element in one's identification.

In fact, Latino men often cannot be neatly categorized in terms of *activo* or *pasivo* because they may switch roles over time or with different partners (Murray, 1990). Carrier (1976a) found that 40% of initially active men and 25% of initially passive men in his Mexican sample had switched roles, depending on the masculinity of their partners. The role taken in the act depends for some on which of the two men is perceived to be more masculine, determining who should play the active role expected of heterosexual men in intercourse.

In summary, homosexual activity that is not too frequent or exclusive and where a passive role is avoided has few implications for one's own sexual identity or the labels applied by others. It is usually when one's sexual activities are exclusively with men, especially playing a passive role, that Latino men come to identify and be identified as homosexual. However, the research also suggests that social workers should not be surprised to find exceptions to these over-simplified organizing principles.

The Structure of Homosexual Opportunity

Research in Latin America finds that homosexual behavior is constrained by economic limitations and the force of family interdependence. Because of these factors, the expansive legal latitude afforded to homosexual conduct in Latin America is substantially eclipsed by a general lack of private space and time (Murray, 1987, 1990; Whitam, 1987; Carrier, 1976a; Adam, 1993). Homes are often crowded with more than one person sleeping in each room. At the same time, many adults cannot afford to live separately from their families (Murray, 1987a; 1990). Middle and upper class men with the economic means to live outside the parental home are nevertheless expected to remain until marriage, and even those who never marry are expected to live with parents or other blood relatives (Murray, 1987).

Although this arrangement may appear stifling, some Latino men indicate a preference for living with their families as a way of avoiding loneliness. In fact, Murray (1987) argues that homosexually involved men work harder than their siblings at maintaining good family relations–to avoid the threat of expulsion from the family and the accompanying loss of security should their homosexual conduct become known. Arboleda (1987) points out that of 60 Peruvian informants, only four had come out to family, and two of them had been thrown out of their homes as a result. Thus, social norms about household formation, family interdependence, and economic solidarity all keep homosexually active men at home, barring marriage.

Latino men may deal with these circumstances in several ways. The most fearful exercise extreme caution about their sexual activity, avoiding being seen with known homosexuals, particularly effeminate men, and avoiding areas where homosexuals are known to congregate (Carrier, 1976b). They may further compensate by greater involvement in heterosexual male activities. However, even those whose homosexuality is an "open secret" use discretion around their families. The effect of these restrictions, according to Murray (1987; 1990) is to push sex "into the streets," making long-term relationships and emotional commitment difficult. With private space at a premium, sexual encounters often take place in public areas, such as restrooms and parks (Taylor, 1986). Likewise, Arboleda (1987) reports that in Peru older men often become desirable as sexual partners simply because (once parents are dead and family economic responsibilities have ebbed) they have more money to spend on the accoutrements that facilitate sex, including drinks and hotel rooms.

This is not to say that some men do not commit to long-term relationships. In the larger urban areas (e.g., San Juan, Buenos Aires, São Paulo or Mexico City) some couples move in together, but they may disguise their relationship by presenting themselves to neighbors and co-workers as cousins or other blood relations. Others find that their families accept the relationship by treating a partner as another son (Murray, 1990). More often, though, homosexual relationships are hidden, or when known, families may create a conspiracy of silence around their son's homosexuality, treating him as if he were heterosexual (Carrier, 1989).

Before supporters of gay liberation bemoan the plight of homosexually-involved men in Latin America, it should be pointed out that there are certain advantages in these norms. Taylor (1986) points out that homosexually involved men in Mexico are not cut off from the rest of society in the way that North American men living in gay enclaves may be. Even gay-identified Mexican men appear more integrated into their families of origin and heterosexual community networks than North American gay men do. In a strongly family-oriented society, they are apparently more able to enjoy the presence of babies, children, and elderly people than are North American gay men.

Latinos also believe that their norms of homosexual conduct are less oriented to sexual consumerism and social segregation than are North American gay male norms (Arguelles & Rich, 1989). And for all their constraints, Latino sexual norms permit all men greater freedom to experiment with homosexuality, which Carrier (1989) speculates they do more frequently in Mexico than in North America. In this regard, sexual attention is likely to be accepted with amusement even on the part of uninterested heterosexual males (Carrier, 1976a). Rather than a separate subculture as in the U.S., there seems to be less of a disjuncture between Latin American homosexual mores and the mores of the larger heterosexual population (Lancaster, 1988).

These comparisons need to be taken cautiously, however, since the gay community in the U.S. has been working increasingly to bridge ethnic and generational gaps as well as rifts between homosexuals and heterosexuals. In the United States it is no longer a foregone conclusion that being gay means giving up the support that families of origin can offer. Likewise, we should not romanticize Latino family life. In spite of their many strengths, Latino families also have negative aspects and for many individual men may not be particularly supportive.

Homosexual Identity Without Gay Community

The norms surrounding family life and homosexual conduct and identity in Latin America constrain not only individual behavior, but also the formation of a collective homosexual or gay identity, a sense of community, and organization for social change. Lancaster (1986) emphasizes that it is not only homophobia that inhibits the rise of a widespread gay liberation movement in Nicaragua. Organization for social change is less common than in the U.S. because the differently constructed sexual norms define fewer people as homosexual and are less marginalizing of those who participate in homosexual conduct. The norms give rise to contradictions between behavior and identity and make public self-identification as homosexual difficult, particularly for masculine men (Murray, 1990). There are no gay ghettoes in Latin America and, in those times and places where censorship has been institutionalized, consciousness-raising media attention has been lacking as well (Murray, 1987; 1990). The problem of maintaining a heterosexual reputation inhibits association and creates conflict between effeminate men and those who are less flamboyant, between those who are out and those still closeted. Such conflict poses huge challenges for leaders who aspire to mobilize homosexually active men (Carrier, 1989). Given these restrictions on "gay" consciousness, identity, and community, Murray (1987; 1990) suggests that Latino men will have to find a different path to liberation than that followed by North American gays.

It should be kept in mind that Latin Americans do not live in a social vacuum; they receive significant exposure to North American and European ideas about sexuality and gayness. Even though the influence of foreign gender and sexual norms has not greatly altered the *activo-pasivo* mentality, the term "gay" has experienced rapid diffusion in Latin America, particularly in urban areas (Lancaster, 1988; Murray & Taylor, 1990). Nevertheless, words often change their meaning as they are imported. For many, the term "gay" has been adopted as a substitute for terms that were already in use such as *entendido* ("in the know") or *de ambiente* ("in the [homosexual] environment") (Lancaster, 1988; Murray & Arboleda; 1987).

But for some, "gay" does reflect a change in the conception of homosexuality. Arboleda (1987) notes that *pasivos* in Peru are more likely to think of themselves as gay, perhaps because gay pride seems to have a special attraction for those whose sexuality and identity are more stigmatized (Adam, 1993). For others, "gay" connotes a "new man" who can enact a *pasivo* role without being a "true" *pasivo* (Murray & Arboleda, 1987); they may also refer to themselves as *modernos* and *internacionales*, terms used in Mexico (and elsewhere) for those who take both roles (Carrier, 1989). There are no universal or consistent understandings of these terms, however, and *activos* still continue to identify as heterosexual (Arboleda, 1987). And while gay ideas are spreading, Murray and Arboleda

(1987) point out that some Mexican liberation organizations avoid the term "gay" because of its cultural imperialist overtones.

Given these ambiguities in labels and underlying identities, the level of organizing for social change, which Whitam (1987) characterizes as low in Brazil, is low only by comparison to North America. We argue that the level of activism and the accomplishments of movement leaders are rather significant. In the largest countries, especially Brazil and Mexico, liberation movements have been active since the 1970s, well before AIDS provided a powerful impetus to activism (Green, 1994; Mott, 1990; Murray & Taylor, 1990). These movements, spurred on in part by the international gay movement, arose in response to anti-homosexual violence and police harassment. The AIDS epidemic also motivated men in countries where there were no organized movements to follow suit with initiatives to combat homophobia, anti-gay violence, and government indifference to AIDS (Green & Asis, 1993; Tielman & Hammelburg, 1993). Schifter (1989) recounts that gay activism in Costa Rica occurred after several pre-conditions for a gay liberation movement had been satisfied during the 1970s: a cultural "generation gap," increasing urbanization, and economic prosperity that reduced the dependence of gay men on their families. The AIDS epidemic gave rise to police raids on gay bars with forced HIV testing. This situation eliminated the shield of anonymity and led homosexually active men to become politicized and to develop a sense of community. The reaction to oppression throughout Latin America has resulted in meetings, protests, publications, pride marches, and the formation of organizations and informal groups in Argentina, Brazil, Costa Rica, Mexico, and numerous other countries (Green, 1994; Green & Asis, 1993; Mott, 1990; Murray & Taylor, 1990; Schifter, 1989).

The achievements have been manifold: cooperative relationships with police in Mexico (Carrier, 1989), positive portrayal of homosexual issues in the media and government cooperation with gay groups for AIDS education in Nicaragua (Adam, 1993; Collinson, 1990), and even endorsement of homosexual rights by a major national party in Peru (Arboleda, 1987).

Knowledge of an international gay liberation movement has given Latin American men some sense of the possibility for change

(Murray, 1990). On the other hand, Whitam (1987), who challenges the idea that action is always better than inaction, argues that homosexuality is less threatening in Latin America precisely because it is not taken too seriously. He asserts that organized activism only turns homosexuality into a political and social threat, with potentially harsh consequences. Because the Latin American conception of homosexuality differs from the North American one, it offers a different set of advantages and disadvantages to men who have sex with men. Thus, the imposition of a North American conception of homosexuality on Latino nations is inappropriate without further information about individual and collective understandings of sexual behavior and identity. Social work interventions based completely on gay understandings of identity and community are likely to lead to distortions of the reality and complexity of the situations faced by many Latino men (Gilmore & Uhl, 1987; Lancaster, 1986).

Furthermore, social work practitioners need to be aware that Latino men in the United States must reconcile the clash of their own understanding about homosexuality with the modern European-American categorization in order to give meaning to their experiences (Almaguer, 1991). Indeed, the level of acculturation in the U.S. has been shown to be an especially important factor in determining Latinos' understandings of their own homosexuality (Magaña & Carrier, 1991).

LATINOS IN THE U.S.

Latinos of Mexican origin make up almost 63% of the total Latino population of the U.S., the next largest groups originating in Puerto Rico (11%) and Cuba (5%) (U.S. Bureau of the Census, 1991). The remaining 21% is divided among other nations of Central and South America and those who claim no national origin. They are concentrated in a handful of states, particularly California, Texas, New York, Florida, Illinois, and the surrounding regions, and they tend to be more urban than the average North American. In general, their levels of education, employment, and income are lower than those of whites for a variety of reasons, including average age, immigration status, geographic location, and language barriers, not to mention discrimination. There are important inter-group differences as well: for example, Cuban-Americans tend to be better off socioeconomically, while Puerto Rican-Americans are the most disadvantaged.

Many Latino men are native to the U.S., but others come because of economic opportunity, and still others migrate to avoid persecution for their homosexuality in their countries of origin or to experience a more open gay life. Homosexual men have sometimes migrated in large numbers: 10,000 to 20,000 migrants in the Mariel boat exodus from Cuba were thought to be homosexual (Arguelles & Rich, 1989; Suarez, 1990). Furthermore, the motivations of migrants shape their residency patterns, whether they come permanently, temporarily, or cross borders repeatedly throughout their lives. Residency status is particularly important to understanding the issues Latino men face as a result of their homosexual behavior or identity, because of the effects that patterns of migration and residency have on the level of acculturation to the U.S. and on the social networks in which Latino men exist.

Acculturation appears to be related to sexual behavior in Latino men. One study found that Latino men in the U.S. were more likely to report bisexual behavior than males from other ethnic or racial groups, and that this behavior was especially common in men born outside the U.S. who had lived here for ten or fewer years (Diaz et al., 1993). However, regardless of birthplace, these same researchers found that Latino males engaging in bisexual behavior were more likely to be currently married than those of any other ethnic group (22% versus an average of 7%). This statistic further supports the notion that homosexually active Latino men are less likely to identify as gay or homosexual, either to themselves or to others, as manifested in their relationships with women.

Trends in HIV-transmission also provide some clues about differences in sexuality between the various Latino sub-populations. There are substantial geographic variations, both in terms of countries of origin and place of residence in the U.S. Almost 50% of the AIDS cases among Latino males born in the United States and the Dominican Republic as well as 65% of cases reported among males born in Cuba, Mexico, Central and South America were related to homosexual behavior (Castro & Manoff, 1988; Marin, 1989; Diaz,

Buehler, & Castro, 1993). At the same time, homosexual transmission (as opposed to transmission through needle sharing) among Latinos tends to be a Western and Southern U.S. phenomenon, more prevalent in Florida, Texas, and California. Latinos in the Northeastern U.S., where more Puerto Ricans reside, tend to be infected more often through needle sharing (for drug use or therapeutic reasons) (Lafferty, Foulk & Ryan, 1990; Marin, 1989). Unfortunately, whether these differences are a result of true population differences in homosexuality, differences in the practice of safer sex, differences in IV-drug use, or some combination of these factors, cannot be determined with these data.

We can only speculate that the varied social networks of Latino men are likely to have differential impacts on sexual attitudes, behaviors, and identity, about which little research has been done. For example, Latino men in the U.S. may live and associate primarily with Anglo gay males, migrant laborers, or extended families. These diverse possibilities need to be considered when doing social work interventions with homosexually active Latino men. With this caveat in mind, we now consider Latino attitudes about homosexuality in comparative perspective with other U.S. ethnic populations, looking at Latino men in varied social contexts in the U.S., including Latino communities, gay communities, and the larger society.

Ethnic Variation in Family Attitudes Toward Homosexuality

Latino families, like other families in the U.S., presuppose a heterosexual orientation and avoid discussion of sexual topics including homosexuality (Morales, 1990). Studies comparing Latinos with other ethnic groups on tolerance of homosexuality show contradictory findings. Ethnic minority communities, including Latinos, are commonly thought to be more conservative, with strict taboos against homosexuality, resulting in the ostracism of homosexual or bisexual men (Honey, 1988; Morales, 1990). Bonilla and Porter (1990) assert that the degree of acculturation is a principal determinant of attitudes, arguing that Latinos may be less tolerant of civil liberties for homosexuals because they are less acculturated to North American values. General Social Survey data of the 1980s showed that as a group Latinos were less supportive than either African-Americans or European-Americans of civil liberties for homosexuals. Bonilla and Porter also point out that variations between Latino populations are important to take into account: Mexican Americans, for instance, are more rural than Puerto Rican Americans and thus likely to espouse more traditional and hostile viewpoints. Whether the differences are due to residence patterns, national origin, or other factors are questions needing further exploration.

In contrast, Alcalay, Sniderman, Mitchell, and Griffin (1989), using a probability sample in California including 104 Latino adults, did not confirm alleged Latino intolerance of homosexuals. Bonilla and Porter (1991) also found that even though Latinos were less tolerant in terms of civil liberties, they were similar to European-Americans in their beliefs about whether homosexuality was acceptable on moral grounds, and in fact were more liberal on this issue than African-Americans. The authors explain this finding by suggesting that the Catholic religion, to which most Latinos subscribe, holds a less rigid and dogmatic position on the morality of homosexuality than many black Protestant churches. Furthermore, Latinos find homosexuality less threatening to the family as an institution than other ethnic groups because of greater flexibility in Latino gender roles. This flexibility may be partly a consequence of the high rate of female paid labor force participation in Latino families, moreso than in many Latin American societies as well.

Another possible explanation is that the Latino extended family system, with its broader networks of support and cooperation, allows individuals more flexibility in their performance of family roles. In contrast, the Anglo nuclear family system provides fewer role alternatives because of smaller family size. As a potential disrupter of rigid and well-defined roles, homosexuality may be perceived as more of a threat to the Anglo family.

Other studies support the perspective that acculturation to North American values is strongly related to attitudes about homosexuality. Newman and Muzzonigro (1993) studied the impact on homophobia of traditional family values about religion, marriage, having children, and speaking a language other than English at home. They found that the stronger the emphasis on traditional values, the less receptive families were toward homosexuality. In addition, the fact that Latino, African American, and Asian American men who are involved in gay communities tend to be highly acculturated (Carrier, 1992; Laird, 1993; Peterson, 1992) reflects more than opportunity; it also indicates that acculturation influences the self-selection of homosexual men of color into gay environments.

When considering the reactions of family members to homosexuality, to speak of Latino families as unitary entities neglects the multiple interconnections that make up extended family networks, where at least some ties are likely to be strong even when others are weak. Indeed, HIV-infected Latino men are highly selective in disclosing their HIV-status: family members who are close and aware of their sexual orientation are more likely to be told (Marks et al., 1992). By utilizing pre-existing social networks and supports, members of Latino families have been effectively mobilized to support Latino gay men with HIV (Kaminsky et al., 1990). This kind of social support acts as a safety net with positive effects on overall health and the immune system of HIV-infected Latino gay men and their significant others. These findings show that Latino families have the potential to be more supportive of their homosexual members than is often acknowledged.

Divided Identities, Divided Loyalties

Apart from family attitudes, homosexually involved Latino men must resolve questions about the implications of their behavior for their own sexual identities and their membership in communities. Morales (1990) asserts that homosexual ethnic minority individuals learn to live in three different communities–ethnic communities, gay communities, and the larger society–each of which fails to support some aspects of the individual's identity. Homosexually involved Latinos face issues of loyalty and belonging to one group over another. These conflicts may inhibit one's ability to adapt and to maximize personal potentials. Sullivan (1993) points out that ethnic minority homosexuals, who experience the isolation of belonging to a hidden community that lies in the intersection of ethnicity and sexual orientation, face bigotry and isolation in the wider gay community and sexual prejudice in their ethnic communities.

Ethnic background may not necessarily constitute a barrier between parents and their gay children (Tremble, Schneider, & Appathurai, 1989), but even those who proudly embrace a gay identity often experience this solution as a trade-off, feeling a loss of connection to their culture. In any case, those who come to identify as gay may have to navigate two acculturation processes, one involving mainstream U.S. culture and the other involving gay culture, sometimes simultaneously. Social workers need to be aware of these distinct possibilities to sort out when each set of issues is salient in interventions with Latino men.

Just how these conflicts of identity and community membership ultimately affect the lives of homosexual Latinos has barely begun to be addressed. By the sheer probability of numbers, they are more likely to couple with men outside their own ethnic group. The search for meaningful relationships with other men may therefore propel Latinos away from their family, community, or ethnic heritage. When partners are found, couples face issues related to the cross-cultural nature of their relationships. These are just a few of the many consequences of the search for identity and community needing further research.

We conclude this section on the interaction of sexuality and ethnicity in the U.S. by noting that there is already evidence that homosexual teenagers of color do encounter special difficulties as a result of their homosexuality, at an age in life when identity formation is a central developmental task. Though Latino-, Asian-, African-, and European-American adolescents report common coming out experiences (Newman & Muzzonigro, 1993), youths of color, including Latinos, are more likely to have serious problems.

In a sample that was 46% Latino gay youths, 41% of the total reported suicide attempts linked to having suffered violence from families, peers, or strangers; 46% of the violent incidents were gay-related (Hunter, 1990). Peterson, Ostrow, and McKirnan (1991) also found clear evidence showing that African-American and Latino gay youths have higher rates of multiple recreational drug use than European-American gay youths, despite the fact that both of these minority populations show equal or lower rates of drug use in the population at large compared to whites (Bachman, Wallace, O'Malley, Johnston, Kurth, & Neighbors, 1991). These statistics underscore the need for services targeted specifically at gay Latino youths as a population at risk.

AIDS AND LATINO ETHNICITY

A responsible and accurate review of the literature on homosexually involved Latino men requires a word about AIDS, if for no other reason, because the literature on Latino men and AIDS outweighs all others. The disturbing level of HIV infection among Latinos warrants concern: by 1990, Latinos and African-Americans accounted for 70% of all the AIDS cases among heterosexual adults and 75% of infant cases in the United States (Lesnick & Pace, 1990). The number of cases of AIDS among Latinos was reported in 1989 as three times that of non-Latino whites; the rate of HIV infection was double the Latino proportion of the population (Castro & Manoff, 1988; Marin, 1989). Higher rates of Latino male bisexuality, spreading HIV through unprotected sex with both men and women, account in part for these high figures (Amaro, 1991; Chu, Peterman, Doll, Buehler, & Curran, 1992; Diaz et al., 1993).

However, these aspects of Latino sexuality and AIDS transmission unfortunately seem to have created an assumed correlation between AIDS and people of color, in particular Latino ethnicity, in the minds of scholars and lay people alike. Careless use of language perpetuates harmful stereotypes, as for example, one study that reported that being Latino is one of the "most consistent predictors of risk behavior" (Doll et al., 1991). Tracing the problem to ethnic background is only likely to offend and alienate those who need services, since after all, ethnicity is not a mutable characteristic.

At the same time, we must recognize that AIDS has complicated the issues faced by all homosexually involved Latino men, HIV-positive or not. Particularly in environments where community leaders blame Latino men having sex with non-Latinos for "bringing infection into the community," identifying and working with this population are not easy tasks. The fact that HIV-positive Latino men seem to experience higher levels of stress and anger related to their homosexuality than non-Latino whites (Ceballos-Capitaine et al., 1990) suggests that clinicians are likely to encounter similar issues for homosexually active Latino men in general.

CONCLUSION

Despite the limitations of focusing only on AIDS in research on homosexually active Latino men, studies of AIDS prevention have yielded important considerations for any program or intervention targeting homosexually active Latino men: socioeconomic status, ethnic prejudices, Latino values such as familialism and personalism, religious and folk beliefs, appropriate language and communication channels, and culturally appropriate services (Carballo-Dieguez, 1989; Kaminsky et al., 1990; Marin, 1989). Taking account of these factors can ensure that Latinos perceive interventions as credible, appropriate, and relevant.

The alternative, applying a majority or mainstream U.S. perspective to the situations of homosexually active Latino men, can only complicate the problems of clients who may be trying to sort out issues of sexual identity. Equating homosexual behavior with identity is clearly an example of this kind of error.

Furthermore, clinicians must be open to encountering differences between the diverse individuals that we put together under the name of "Latinos," particularly when dealing with issues about homosexuality. Likewise, the term "gay," with all of its special sociological and political connotations, may not be at all relevant to Latino male homosexual experience. When a client uses the word "gay," even as a self-referent, probing his conception of gayness might reveal significant differences from what the social worker has in mind.

Therefore, it is important to assist the client in searching for his own understanding of his sexuality and the implications it will have for his relationships with family, ethnic community, and the gay community. Latino men may face economic and family constraints on their behavior that make adoption of a homosexual or gay identity especially risky. Practitioners should be careful not to underestimate the importance of discretion and the special risks of coming out in a Latino context. Even those highly acculturated men who adopt a gay identity may experience discomfort with gay community norms encouraging sexual consumerism as well as prejudices against people of color. Recognizing the tensions between competing identities and communities may help clients clarify these issues and feel validated in both their ethnic and sexual identities.

Finally, social workers need to be alert to the fact that involvement in certain activities, such as violent behavior (whether perpetrator or target), chemical substance abuse, or suicide attempts, may merely be masking underlying difficulties that a client is having with his sexuality.

In spite of the need for research on these and other core issues of sexual behavior and identity, the trend in scholarship on homosexually active Latino men is to focus increasingly on AIDS issues to the exclusion of other areas. Recent research on Latino men who have sex with men that does not deal exclusively with AIDS is scarce. We have purposely avoided reinforcing this trend by emphasizing other literatures and drawing on AIDS research when it serves to illustrate larger points about attitudes, behaviors, identities, and communities.

More research on the social context and implications of Latino sexual behavior, identities, and communities is needed to understand how both Anglo and Latino cultural life are experienced by Latino men who have sex with men. Because our current understanding of these sociocultural issues is rudimentary at best, this program of research would incidentally provide invaluable insights in the fight against AIDS as well.

By thus putting the horse back in front of the cart, as it were, we can also improve our understanding of the differential consequences of a variety of sociocultural contexts on self-esteem, health, and positive identity formation, to name just a few of the myriad possibilities. The importance of this body of theory and research to Latino gay men, Latino communities, and gay communities is obvious, but its relevance extends far beyond them: it has significance for social work practice with other ethnic populations, families with gay members, and community organizing and advocacy for social change.

REFERENCES

Adam, B. D. (1993). In Nicaragua: Homosexuality without a gay world. *Journal of Homosexuality, 24*(3/4), 171-181.
Alcalay, R., Sniderman, P. M., Mitchell, J., & Griffin, R. (1989). Ethnic differences in knowledge of AIDS transmission and attitudes towards gays and

people with AIDS. *International Quarterly of Community Health Education,*
10(3), 213-222.

Almaguer, T. (1991). A cartography of homosexual identity and behavior. *Differ-*
ences, 3(2), 75-100.

Amaro, H. (1991). AIDS/HIV among Hispanics in the Northeast and Puerto Rico:
Report of findings and recommendations. *Migration World Magazine, 19*(4),
23-29.

Arboleda, M. (1987). Social attitudes and sexual variance in Lima. In S. O. Murray
(Ed.), *Male homosexuality in Central and South America* (pp. 101-117). New
York: Gay Academic Union.

Arguelles, L., & Rich, B. R. (1989). Homosexuality, homophobia, and revolution:
Notes toward an understanding of the Cuban lesbian and gay male experience.
In M. B. Duberman, M. Vicinus, & G. Chauncey (Eds.), *Hidden from history:*
Reclaiming the gay and lesbian past (pp. 441-455). New York: Meridian
Books.

Bachman, J. G., Wallace, J. M., O'Malley, P. M., Johnston, L. D., Kurth, C. L., &
Neighbors, H. W. (1991). Racial/ethnic differences in smoking, drinking, and
illicit drug use among American high school seniors, 1976-89. *American Jour-*
nal of Public Health, 81(3), 372-377.

Bonilla, L. & Porter, J. (1990). A comparison of Latino, black, and non-Hispanic
white attitudes toward homosexuality. *Hispanic Journal of Behavioral Sciences,*
12(4), 437-452.

Carballo-Dieguez, A. (1989). Hispanic culture, gay male culture, and AIDS:
Counseling implications. *Journal of Counseling and Development, 68*(1),
26-30.

Carrier, J. M. (1976a). Cultural factors affecting urban Mexican male homosexual
behavior. *Archives of Sexual Behavior, 5*, 103-124.

Carrier, J. M. (1976b). Family attitudes and Mexican male homosexuality. *Urban*
Life, 5(3). 359-375.

Carrier, J. M. (1989). Gay liberation and coming out in Mexico. *Journal of*
Homosexuality, 17(3/4), 225-252.

Carrier, J. M. (1992). Miguel: Sexual life history of a gay Mexican-American. In
G. Herdt (Ed.), *Gay culture in America: Essays from the field* (pp. 202-224).
Boston: Beacon Press.

Castro, K. G., & Manoff, S. B. (1988). The epidemiology of AIDS in Hispanic
adolescents. In M. Quackenbush, & M. Nelson. (Eds.), *The AIDS challenge:*
Prevention education for young people (pp. 321-331). Santa Cruz, CA: Network Publications.

Ceballos-Capitaine, A., Szapocznik, J., Blaney, N. T., Morgan, R. O., Millon, C., &
Eisdorfer, C. (1990). Ethnicity, emotional distress, stress-related disruption,
and coping among HIV seropositive gay males. *Hispanic Journal of Behavior-*
al Sciences, 12(2), 135-152.

Chu, S. Y., Peterman, T. A., Doll, L. S., Buehler, J. W., & Curran, J. W. (1992).
AIDS in bisexual men in the United States: Epidemiology and transmission to
women. *American Journal of Public Health, 82*(2), 220-224.

Collinson, H. (1990). The home front: Family life and sexuality. In H. Collinson (Ed.), *Women and revolution in Nicaragua* (pp. 8-27). London: Zed Books.

de la Garza, R. O., Falcon, A., Garcia, F. C., & Garcia, J. A. (1992). *Latino nation political survey: Summary of findings*. Boulder, CO: Westview Press.

d'Emilio, J. (1983). *Sexual politics, sexual communities*. Chicago: University of Chicago Press.

Diaz, T., Buehler, J. W., Castro, K. G., & Ward, J. W. (1993). AIDS trends among Hispanics in the United States. *American Journal of Public Health*, 83(4), 504.

Diaz, T., Chu, S. Y., Frederick, M., Hermann, P., Levy, A., Mokotoff, E., Whyte, B., Conti, L., Herr, M., Checko, P. J., Rietmeijer, C.A., Sorvillo, F., & Mukhtar, Q. (1993). Sociodemographics and HIV risk behaviors of bisexual men with AIDS: Results from a multistate interview project. *AIDS*, 7(9), 1227-1232.

Doll, L. S., Byers, R. H., Bolan, G., Douglas, J. M. Jr., Moss, P. M., Weller, P. D., Joy, D., Barthjolow, B. N., & Harrison, J. S. (1991). Homosexual men who engage in high-risk sexual behavior: A multicenter comparison. *Sexually Transmitted Diseases*, 18(3), 170-175.

Doll, L. S., Petersen, L. R., White, C. R., Johnson, E. S. & Ward, J. W. (1992). Homosexually and nonhomosexually identified men who have sex with men: A behavioral comparison. *Journal of Sex Research*, 29(1), 1-14.

Gilmore, D. D., & Uhl, S. C. (1987). A man or not a man? A history of male homosexuality. *Sociologisch-Tijdschrift*, 14(4), 620-644.

Green, J., & Asis, E. (1993). Gays and lesbians: the closet door swings open. *Report on the Americas*, 26(4), 4-8.

Green, J. N. (1994). The emergence of the Brazilian gay liberation movement, 1977-1981. *Latin American Perspectives*, 21(1), 39.

Honey, E. (1988). AIDS and the inner city: Critical issues. *Social Casework*, 69(6), 365-370.

Hunter, J. (1990). Violence against lesbian and gay male youths. *Journal of Interpersonal Violence*, 5(3), 295-300.

Icard, L. (1986). Black men and conflicting social identities. In J. Gripton & M. Valentich (Eds.), *Social work practice in sexual problems*. New York: The Haworth Press, Inc.

Kaminsky, S., Kurtines, W., Hervis, O. O., Blaney, N. T., Millon, C., & Szapocznik, J. (1990). Life enhancement counseling with HIV infected Hispanic gay males. *Hispanic Journal of Behavioral Sciences*, 12(2), 177-195.

Lafferty, J., Foulk, D., & Ryan, R. (1990). Needle sharing for the use of therapeutic drugs as a potential AIDS risk behavior among migrant Hispanic farmworkers in the Eastern stream. *International Quarterly of Community Health Education*, 11(2), 135-143.

Laird, J. (1993). Lesbian and gay families. In F. Walsh (Ed.), *Normal family processes* (pp. 282-328). New York: Guilford Press.

Lancaster, R. N. (1986). Comment on Arguelles and Rich's "Homosexuality, homophobia, and revolution: Notes toward an understanding of the Cuban lesbian and gay male experiences: II." *Signs*, 12(1), 188-192.

Lancaster, R. N. (1988). Subject honor and object shame: The construction of male homosexuality and stigma in Nicaragua. *Ethnology, 27*(2), 111-125.

Lesnick, H., & Pace, B. (1990). Knowledge of AIDS risk factors in South Bronx minority college students. *Journal of Acquired Immune Deficiency Syndrome, 3*(2), 173-176.

Magaña, J. R., & Carrier, J. M. (1991). Mexican and Mexican American male sexual behavior and the spread of AIDS in California. *Journal of Sex Research, 28*(3), 425-441.

Marin, G. (1989). AIDS prevention among Hispanics: Needs, risk behaviors, and cultural values. *Public Health Report, 104*(5), 411-415.

Marks, G., Bundek, N. I., Richardson, J. L., Ruiz, M. S., Maldonado, N., & Mason, H. R. (1992). Self-disclosure of HIV infection: Preliminary results from a sample of Hispanic men. *Health Psychology, 11*(5), 300-306.

Morales, E. S. (1990). HIV infection and Hispanic gay and bisexual men. *Hispanic Journal of Behavioral Sciences, 12*(2), 212-222.

Mott, L. (1990). Brazil. In W. R. Dynes (Ed.), *Encyclopedia of Homosexuality, 1* (pp. 162-164). New York: Garland Publishing, Inc.

Murray, S. O. (1987). The family as an obstacle to the growth of a gay subculture in Latin America. In S. O. Murray (Ed.), *Male homosexuality in Central and South America* (pp. 118-129). New York: Gay Academic Union.

Murray, S. O., & Arboleda, G. (1987). Stigma transformation and relexification: "Gay" in Latin America. In S. O. Murray (Ed.), *Male homosexuality in Central and South America* (pp. 130-138). New York: Gay Academic Union.

Murray, S. O. (1990). Latin America. In W. R. Dynes (Ed.), *Encyclopedia of homosexuality, 1* (pp. 678-681). New York: Garland Publishing, Inc.

Murray, S. O., & Taylor, C. L. (1990). Mexico. In W. R. Dynes (Ed.), *Encyclopedia of homosexuality, 2* (pp. 803-807). New York: Garland Publishing, Inc.

Newman, B. S., & Muzzonigro, P. G. (1993). The effects of traditional family values on the coming out process of gay male adolescents. *Adolescence, 28*(109), 213-226.

Peterson, J. L. (1992). Black men and their same-sex desires and behaviors. In G. Herdt (Ed.), *Gay culture in America: Essays from the field* (pp. 147-164). Boston: Beacon Press.

Peterson, P. L., Ostrow, D. G., & McKirnan, D. J. (1991). Behavioral interventions for the primary prevention of HIV infection among homosexual and bisexual men. *Journal of Primary Prevention, 12*(1), 19-34.

Schifter, J. (1989). *La formación de una contracultura: Homosexualismo y SIDA en Costa Rica*. San José, Costa Rica: Ediciones Guayacán.

Suarez, P. J. (1990). Cuba. In W. R. Dynes (Ed.), *Encyclopedia of homosexuality, 1* (pp. 285-287). New York: Garland Publishing, Inc.

Sullivan, T. (1993, February 26). A double-edged sword: Finding a place in the world can be difficult for minority gays. *Fort Worth Star Telegram*, p. 1.

Taylor, C. L. (1986). Mexican male homosexual interaction in public contexts. *Journal of Homosexuality, 11*(3/4), 117-136.

Tielman, R., & Hammelburg, H. (1993). World survey on the social and legal position of gays and lesbians. In A. Hendriks, R. Tielman, & E. van der Veen (Eds.), *The third pink book: A global view of lesbian and gay liberation and oppression* (pp. 249-342). Buffalo, NY: Prometheus Books.

Tremble, B., Schneider, M., & Appathurai, C. (1989). Growing up gay or lesbian in a multicultural context. In G. Herdt (Ed.), *Gay and lesbian youth* (pp. 253-264). New York: The Haworth Press, Inc.

United States Bureau of the Census. (1991). Current Population Reports, Series P-20, No. 455. *The Hispanic Population in the United States: March 1991.* Washington, DC: United States Government Publications Office.

Whitam, F. (1987). Os entendidos: Gay life in São Paulo. In S. O. Murray (Ed.), *Male homosexuality in Central and South America* (pp. 24-54). New York: Gay Academic Union.

Understanding Filipino Male Homosexuality:
Implications for Social Services

Felix I. Rodriguez

SUMMARY. This paper draws on research as well as the observations of the author to examine homosexual behavior and identity in the Philippines within the context of historical and contemporary attitudes toward homosexuality and gender relations. It moves on to explore the implications of cultural expectations on Filipinos in the United States, especially with regard to how they might adapt to American culture and society. The paper ends with suggestions for providing ethnically sensitive services to homosexually active Filipino men. *[Article copies available from The Haworth Document Delivery Service: 1-800-342-9678. E-mail address: getinfo@haworth.com]*

This paper is about Filipino gay men in America. First, it considers homosexual behavior and identity in Philippine society. Second, it examines gender relations and social attitudes toward homosexuality in the Philippines. Third, it looks at homosexuality among Filipinos in the United States and how it relates to the question of identity in an adopted culture. Lastly, it offers suggestions to social work practitioners for working with Filipino gay men.

Felix I. Rodriguez, PhD, is Research Coordinator, University of Washington, School of Social Work, Social Development Research Group, 146 North Canal Street, Suite 211, Seattle, WA 98103.

[Haworth co-indexing entry note]: "Understanding Filipino Male Homosexuality: Implications for Social Services." Rodriguez, Felix I. Co-published simultaneously in *Journal of Gay & Lesbian Social Services* (The Haworth Press, Inc.) Vol. 5, No. 2/3, 1996, pp. 93-113; and: *Men of Color: A Context for Service to Homosexually Active Men* (ed: John F. Longres) The Haworth Press, Inc., 1996, pp. 93-113; and: *Men of Color: A Context for Service to Homosexually Active Men* (ed: John F. Longres) Harrington Park Press, an imprint of The Haworth Press, Inc., 1996, pp. 93-113. Single or multiple copies of this article are available from The Haworth Document Delivery Service [1-800-342-9678, 9:00 a.m. - 5:00 p.m. (EST). E-mail address: getinfo@haworth.com].

The paper draws on the observations of the author as well as on the relatively few, but nevertheless rich, published works on homosexual behavior among Filipino men in the Philippines and the United States by other researchers. Foremost among these is Hart's article (1968) which, although admittedly exploratory, is useful in understanding local beliefs about homosexuality. Nery's (1979) work describes the subculture of male prostitutes who cater mainly to a homosexual clientele in Metropolitan Manila. Mathews' investigation (1987a,b) touches on the motivation of male prostitutes. Whitam's recent article (1992) examines heterosexual and homosexual contact in the Philippines, which raises an important theoretical issue on homosexual behavior and identity. Murray (1992) presents observations made by Spanish chroniclers of persons analogous to the *berdache*. Itiel (1989) offers vivid observations on gay life in the Philippines. In the United States, articles have dealt with lives of Filipino gays (De Guzman, 1989a; 1992), the experience of coming-out (Orquiola, 1992), writing by immigrant gay men (Manalansan, 1993), and AIDS among Filipino gay men (De Guzman, 1989b; Pimentel, 1990; Silva, 1992).

DEFINING HOMOSEXUALITY IN FILIPINO CULTURE

To understand Filipino gay men in America, we must begin in the Philippines. Those who came to America as adults may not easily fit into the categories of "straight," "homosexual," or "bisexual." They are likely to have been socialized into patterns which, although perhaps understandable through American terms, represent a different social construction of homosexuality. Even Filipinos born in the United States may have identities closer to traditional Filipino mores.

Homosexual behavior and identity as shaped by local, national, and transnational forces vary across space and time. Like all societies, cultural mores and traditions in the Philippines are continually evolving. Today, at least three representations of homosexual conduct and identity are visible. One, the *bakla*, refers to men assuming the gender of a woman. This type conforms to Greenberg's (1988) description of transgenderal homosexuality. The second includes call-boys and heterosexual men who "trade" their masculinity for money and other favors (Nery, 1979; Mathews, 1987a,b). These men do not consider themselves homosexual because they generally take the masculine role in a relationship with a *bakla*. The *bakla* and the homosexually active heterosexual male represent the two traditional ways homosexual conduct has been institutionalized in the Philippines.

The third type represents a pattern similar to Greenberg's (1988) description of egalitarian homosexuality. One sees in the Philippines two males, neither of whom is effeminate, forming a homosexual union without regard to pre-defined masculine or feminine roles. Although it may not be exactly new, there is no doubt that American gay lifestyle, if there is such a notion, has influenced this pattern of homosexual behavior. Thus, these men tend to be more westernized and are likely to call themselves "gay," which may not preclude others from regarding them as *bakla*. Although these three representations are visible in the Philippines, the *bakla* and call-boys have been studied most. For this reason and because they are considered the traditional forms, this section will give primary attention to the *bakla* and call-boy.

Bakla

The word homosexual, as it is understood in contemporary Western societies, has no direct translation in Filipino. In Tagalog language, *bakla* traditionally refers to a man who acts like a woman. Using the Filipino system of word-building, it can be transformed into *kabaklaan*, which means the state of being a *bakla*. A *bakla* views his identity as that of a pseudo-woman, i.e., a man with a female heart (Manalansan, 1990). He represents a third gender: one half a man, the other half a woman. Thus, others may refer to *bakla* as "hap-hap" (half-half) or *balaki*, a combination of *lalaki* (man or boy) and *babae* (girl or woman). Filipinos also use *binabae* which means a man who has feminine qualities.

Although the word *bakla* refers to a man who is feminine, it is not uncommon for men who deviate from traditional concepts of masculinity to be labeled as such. Filipinos generally expect males to be masculine, i.e., men are supposed to marry and have children. A man who deviates from this rule is suspected of being a *bakla*. An adult male who is simply refined and has no preference for the same sex may be labeled as *"parang babae"* (like a woman) and may be considered a *bakla*. An English writer who spent a few years in a desolate village in eastern Luzon reports that people in the community thought he was *bakla* because he was not married at his age and was living alone without a woman (Hamilton-Paterson, 1987).

Bakla signifies an identification with the female gender. Effeminacy marks the *bakla*'s self-presentation which may border on flamboyance, although not all *bakla* are effeminate. *Bakla* commonly practice cross-dressing, although not all *bakla* are cross-dressers. Moreover, *bakla* have developed their own norms of proper behavior. Sex between *bakla* is viewed as undesirable. A *bakla* expresses his disgust for such a relation by saying *"baka tamaan ako ng kidlat"* (I might be hit by lightning if I have sex with another *bakla*). They avoid having sexual relations with each other in much the same way as two effeminate gays in the United States would call themselves "sisters." *Bakla* use an expression which applies to men who engage in homosexual relations but present themselves as masculine or straight. In *bakla* argot, they are referred to as men who refuse to take off their cloak (*"ayaw magladlad ng kapa"*). This is perhaps the equivalent of "being in the closet." In the Filipino context, however, not taking off one's cloak does not mean that one refuses to admit that he is homosexual. Rather, it means that one refuses to recognize he is *bakla,* i.e., he is a pseudo-woman who is expected to act and behave like one.

Men may engage in homosexual conduct but would not consider themselves *bakla* because they do not assume the identity of a pseudo-woman. What one expects to do in the sex act determines who is *bakla* and who is not. The word "expects" needs to be stressed because expectations may occasionally be broken without necessarily altering the way men understand themselves. In fellatio, for instance, the one who is expected to take the role of the fellator is considered *bakla*. The partner who expects to be fellated is considered straight or a real man. Similarly, in anal intercourse, the partner who is expected to take the passive role is considered *bakla* while the one who takes the active role is not. Thus, men who expect to be fellated or assume the inserter role in anal intercourse are not considered by others or by themselves to be *bakla*. Being *bakla* connotes a specific role and behavior in same sex relations and, at least for the one assuming the masculine role, has nothing to do with the object of sexual arousal.

A *bakla* generally prefers straight men. Hence, it is essential that he finds willing sex partners. It is well-known that *bakla* may resort to call-boys for sex, but this is not the only way they fulfill their sexual needs. With some degree of success, *bakla* are able to find straight men, other than call-boys, who are not averse to having sexual relations with a *bakla*. Some straight men are willing to have sex with *bakla*, probably because they do not consider it a threat to their masculinity. In other societies, a straight man who has sex with a *bakla*, who is still a male after all, would be considered bisexual. In the Philippines, as long as men do not assume the feminine role in sex, they are considered straight by definition. Filipino society has circumscribed masculinity in broad terms which raises an important issue of what it means to be a heterosexual male in the Philippines. Does part of being male in Filipino society include playing the masculine role in same-sex relations? Studies have reported that heterosexual males feel that having sex with *bakla* enhances their masculinity (Hart, 1968; Mathews, 1987a). Thus, it is not surprising to find married men who continue to have sex with *bakla*. Some may even have the approval of their wives.

The call-boy or the male prostitute is often associated with the *bakla* (Manalansan, 1990). Previous research has examined the call-boy subculture especially in big cities (Nery, 1979; Mathews, 1987a; 1987b). Call-boys attribute their "hustling" to poverty and economic need (Mathews, 1987a; 1987b). Whitam (1992) views the relationship between call-boys and *bayot* (equivalent of *bakla* in Cebuano language) as a heterosexual-homosexual contact with its own logic. Call-boys usually work in bars either as "exotic" dancers or so-called hosts. They are expected to take the masculine role in sex and, therefore, do not consider themselves *bakla*. However, it is not uncommon for a call-boy to become a *bakla* which may eventually diminish his masculinity. When it happens, he is no longer considered desirable because a *bakla* is not attractive to another *bakla*.

The relationship between call-boy and *bakla* is built on a system where sex is exchanged for anything that can be of help to the call-boy, whether it is cash, clothes, vacation, or being temporarily or permanently kept. Foreign gay tourists report that Filipino call-boys do not directly ask for money as remuneration for sex (Itiel, 1989). They may say that they need money for their education, for a sick relative, or for their family. In many instances, a *bakla* meets a call-boy or another man who becomes a constant companion or long-term partner. It is understood that the *bakla* will provide materially in exchange for the sex the male partner gives. A *bakla* may refer to his partner as *asawa* (husband). Typically, the *bakla* is older and takes care of the younger partner. If the partner marries, it is not unusual to find some *bakla* providing for the wife and children as well.

HOMOSEXUALITY AND SOCIAL ATTITUDES

Scholars and travel writers alike have been amazed by the tolerant attitude of Filipinos toward homosexual behavior. Laws criminalizing homosexual acts do not exist. Whitam and Mathy (1986), in their classification of national attitudes toward homosexuality, consider Filipinos to be "very tolerant." They also report that tolerance and amusement are common responses to doll-playing and cross-dressing in "pre-homosexual" children. Filipino mothers are not usually scandalized by cross-gender behavior. They may even collaborate with an effeminate child by keeping it a secret from their husbands (Whitam and Mathy, 1986).

Authors have offered various explanations for this favorable attitude. Some focus on the Filipino belief that *bakla* is regarded as a natural part of life and that every family is bound to have one (Hart, 1968; Whitam and Mathy, 1986; Mathews, 1987b). According to Hart (1968), rural Filipinos are accepting of *bayot* because they are believed to be hereditary. Parents of effeminate boys, therefore, may encourage them to be *bakla* or cross-dressers. Favorable attitudes toward same-sex friendships indicate that homosexuality is not regarded as deviant behavior (Hart, 1968). Filipino males are generally seen touching each other or with hands around each other's shoulders. Such behavior, which is also common among girls and women, is not frowned upon.

Beliefs about the natural origin of *bakla* and the perception that homosexuality is not a deviant behavior may explain the tolerant attitude of Filipinos toward *bakla*. However, a *bakla* may still be an object of ridicule, which indicates that this perceived tolerance is actually misleading. Filipinos may be tolerant of homosexual behavior but it does not mean that the *bakla* is generally regarded with respect. It is not uncommon to find a *bakla* being taunted and physically abused by friends and even complete strangers. Some men fear being found out they are *bakla* because of rejection by family and humiliation by friends.

Whitam (1992) explains that tolerance may be partly due to the size and density of the Philippine population. High population density encourages people to tolerate one another. Gays and lesbians who publicly display their behavior will be tolerated as heterosexual people become desensitized. In the process, homosexuality is demystified. This explanation, however, may be true only for urban localities and big cities where high population density and crowding are common. It does not account for positive attitudes toward the *bakla* in smaller towns and rural villages where population density is lower.

The attitude toward the *bakla* is, at best, ambiguous or mixed. They may be tolerated but are harassed and victimized as well (Manalansan, 1990). An explanation for this mixed attitude may be found in the broader system of gender relations and the changes it has undergone as a result of colonization. On the one hand, since the *bakla* typically identifies with the female gender, the positive attitude of Filipinos may be an extension of the esteem accorded to women in the Philippines. Whitam and Mathy (1986) have recognized that the prominent role of women in the present and in the past may exert a "softening effect" on societal attitudes toward the *bayot*, although they do not explain why this is so. The negative attitude toward the *bakla*, on the other hand, may be attributed to factors which altered gender relations and, therefore, weakened women's position. Hence, it is important to examine the change in gender relations over time and how it influenced attitudes toward the *bakla*.

Historical research reveals that Southeast Asian women have enjoyed a status of high autonomy and economic importance even with the growing influence of Islam, Buddhism, Confucianism, and Christianity (Reid, 1988). The Philippines may appear westernized to a casual observer, but Filipinos are Southeast Asians first and foremost. They, therefore, possess many of the traditional gender role expectations associated with Southeast Asian culture and ecology. Settlements in the Philippines, before the encounter with Ferdinand Magellan in 1521, grew around river tributaries and other bodies of water. A riverine, maritime culture built on trade with neighboring islands had developed where men specialized in navigation and women engaged in trade and marketing. Women became known as shrewd traders. Then as now, they are keepers of the household purse. In the interior, where wet rice cultivation formed the basic economy, women played essential roles ranging from planting and harvesting to marketing.

The strong position of women in pre-colonized Philippines also extended to non-material spheres. In the Visayas, women priests known as *babaylan* played an important role in linking the material world with spirits who ruled over nature. Spanish chronicles generally regarded native priests as sorcerers and instruments of the devil (Blair & Robertson, 1903; 1904). It is not impossible that many of them could have been killed upon the orders of Spanish friars. Aside from their spiritual function, women were also known as healers. Because they were believed to be the source of life, women were highly regarded for their mystical and magical powers.

The autonomy of women can be seen in sexual relations and control over fertility as well. Spanish chronicles reveal that men implanted metal objects under the skin of their penis in order to satisfy women (Reid, 1988). The tradition was justified by the belief that women preferred men who had penile implants. With respect to fertility, Visayan women were known to practice abortion in order to control family size (Reid, 1988).

The economic and social importance of women in Philippine society from pre-colonization up to the present may account for the positive attitudes toward the *bakla*. Since the *bakla* is believed to be pseudo-woman and women have a strong position in society, a man who switches gender does not diminish his status. The influence of equal status of men and women on attitude toward gender switching can also be found in other cultures. Greenberg (1988) cites the case of the Hopis where men's and women's roles, although distinct, are complementary and equal. A man abandoning his sex for the female gender is not regarded as having diminished status. This is in contrast with New Guinea, where men do not consider women as equals, and a man who switches gender is regarded as inferior (Greenberg, 1988).

Negative attitudes toward the *bakla* as demonstrated in taunting and physical violence may stem from colonization which transformed gender relations. For over three centuries (1571-1898), Spain promoted, in a Southeast Asian culture, a Catholic theology which upheld the superiority of men over women. Masculinity came to be viewed as the ability to subjugate women. Women's role became secondary, not complementary, to men. The American occupation (1898-1946) reinforced the Western notion of masculinity ingrained during the Spanish period. It led to further degradation of Filipino women. The military bases of the United States promoted a sex industry which prostituted a great number of Filipino women. As a result of Spanish and American colonization, feelings toward the *bakla* may have changed. On the one hand, colonization seriously degraded women's status. Therefore, to switch from masculine to feminine has become degrading as well. On the other hand, colonization gave masculinity higher value and, therefore, the *bakla*, who is only half a man, is not exactly a man. The *bakla* has become the reflection of women's lower position and the representation of failed manhood.

CULTURE, HISTORY, AND SEXUAL IDENTITY: BEING GAY AND FILIPINO IN AMERICA

Anxieties and Their Sources

In the U.S. in 1990, persons of Filipino descent numbered 1,407,000, representing an increase of nearly 83 percent from 775,000 in 1980 (U.S. Bureau of the Census, 1993). There are Filipinos who have lived in the United States for generations while there are those who have recently immigrated. This population includes the young, the old, married, and unmarried adults. Professional and occupational skills vary. Filipinos are nurses, medical technicians, doctors, postal workers, data entry clerks, teachers, businesspeople, etc. They also reflect a range of sexual orientations from those inclined to be *bakla* to homosexually active heterosexuals to modern gays.

Regardless of sexual orientation, being Filipino presents various problems. Although they experience many typical immigrant problems, their special relationship with the United States presents some unique dilemmas. The Philippines was an American colony for nearly fifty years. Filipinos have always believed that the United States is a friend to them and that they share the same values of democracy, justice, and freedom—global concepts that have now become cliches. Because of their belief in this "special relationship," Filipinos expect that they will be treated in America with some degree of respect and accommodation. They also expect that since their Western education gives them a fairly good degree of competence in American culture, their adjustment will not be as difficult compared to other groups. However, Filipinos are disappointed when their feelings for the United States and their expectations are not reciprocated with equal interest. Stories abound of Filipinos who are shocked to find out that Americans generally do not know about the Philippines. And when they do, their knowledge is limited to horrible stories of greedy dictators, poverty, and underdevelopment. Filipinos are hurt when Americans complain about their accent since most of them believe they possess a fair degree of skill in English and can be easily understood.

American attitudes toward people of other races present some challenges for Filipinos. They have to deal with racism whether at work or in their local communities, in both its subtle and blatant forms. They have to deal with the status of being the colonized, of being objectified, of being the "other" in an unequal relationship. Because of colonization, Filipinos are almost always put on the defensive when they are perceived by others to be Western yet not Western enough, or Asian yet not Asian enough. Filipinos end up apologizing for their own culture, for traits they both lack and possess. Like most of those who have been colonized, Filipinos try desperately to resemble their colonizer, hoping it will be easier for them to be accepted and, hence, improve their status. Yet, they never assimilate completely because the dominant culture permits it only up to a certain point. Thus, they live what Memmi (1967) calls a life of "painful and constant ambiguity." Filipinos, like people from other groups, are status conscious. Their identity as individuals is strongly linked with factors which define their status, such as family name, occupation, wealth, kinship, and the social status of their friends and relatives. Filipino identity is largely defined and shaped by community. Thus, resettling in the Unites States, where identity is self-constructed and social status is measured by individual accomplishments, can make life difficult for Filipinos. Probably it is the loss of identity and status that causes anxieties among many Filipinos, aside from the common problems of maintaining jobs and relationships. Filipinos have to adjust to a culture where individualism is valued and where people are supposed to take charge of their own lives. Moreover, they have to cope with the fact that they are only one of the many who are claiming a space in the landscape of American political economy, along with African-Americans, Mexican-Americans, Chinese-Americans, Japanese-Americans, Korean-Americans, Native-Americans, and others.

Aside from adjusting to another culture, Filipinos in the United States have to deal with problems within their own community. (I use the term community to refer to ethnic affiliation, not as a political or geographic construct.) Divisions within the Filipino community are traceable to interrelated social, economic, and cultural cleavages that exist in the Philippines. Filipino society remains "semi-feudal" and "semi-colonial." (For a detailed analysis, see Guerrero, 1971.) Differences among social classes and their respective interests are sharp. A number of families and their retainers control the larger share of the nation's wealth, leaving very little to the rest who are poor, nearly poor, and barely surviving. A political culture shaped by a weak sense of nationhood supports this structure. Powerful regional elites representing their own economic interests compete for national control over the country's resources. Family and kin are more important than nation. National politics can become an extension of competition among wealthy families for economic power. Favors are bartered and exchanged. One's status and wealth shape all levels of social relations. Rosca (1987) has noted that "since rigid relations, based on property, precluded innovation and creativity, the society has little use for intelligent people."

Another division stems from colonization. The superimposition of Western attitudes with indigenous Southeast Asian values has created polar cultural orientations. A Great Cultural Divide (Enriquez, Herrera, & Tubayan, 1991) separates those with a stronger Western orientation from those who are more native, although most fall within a continuum of these polarities. Some are more Western and less Southeast Asian while others are more Southeast Asian and less western in orientation. Preference for western culture remains very strong, however, owing to the influence of American media. It is stronger among the westernized elites who have the wherewithal to travel and import trends and ideas from abroad (Enriquez, Herrera, & Tubayan, 1991). However, interest in promoting indigenous perspectives has been sustained despite strong western influences. In the social sciences, a movement called Sikolohiyang Pilipino (Filipino Psychology) has corrected wrong interpretations of Filipino behavior by western writers and scholars (Enriquez, 1993; 1994). It has helped Filipinos to see themselves on their own terms.

In many ways, the divisions found in the so-called Filipino-American community are only an extension of cleavages in the Philippines. In Southern California, which has the largest concentration of Filipinos in the United States, there are more than four hundred organizations based on regional, religious, and social divisions. They represent various combinations of class membership, regional loyalty, and cultural orientation. There are immigrants from powerful land-owning classes. There are those who are university-educated and highly skilled (although they may not have jobs commensurate with their experience and education). And there are those who come from the ranks of rural peasants, the uneducated, and the hopelessly poor.

Immigrants bring their own values and prejudices. The Tagalogs are distrustful of Ilokanos. The Cebuanos are not happy with what they perceive as the domination of Tagalog-speaking Manileños. Furthermore, differences also exist between those who have been born in the United States and those who are recent immigrants—the division between Fil-im (Filipino immigrant) and Fil-am (Filipino-American). Filipino-Americans, who have lived here for two or three generations, feel that they are not appreciated by recent Filipino immigrants for paving their way in America. On the other hand, recent immigrants, because they are only beginning to acculturate in mainstream America, feel that Filipino-Americans are ashamed to identify with them.

Most Filipinos still entertain the idea of going home and are seriously concerned with those they have left behind. In fact, immigration is seen as a means of improving one's lot and helping those who remain in the Philippines. To most Filipinos who live here, life in the United States, despite its difficulties, is still a lot better compared to poverty and economic hardships in the Philippines. However, to those who are more economically successful than others, the status of the Philippines as a poor Third World country is like a bad memory from the past. Successful Filipinos are upset that the status they have achieved in the United States does not prevent others from associating them with a country that is submerged in centuries of economic deprivation. To others outside of their own community, Filipino identity is inseparable from their country's history.

Attitude Toward Homosexuals in the Filipino-American Community

The homosexually active Filipino is a product of all the economic and cultural contradictions of his society. He has to deal with conflicts arising from divisions within his community. He has to face problems which stem from being an ethnic minority and homosexual. Within his own community, he has to deal with Filipino-American attitudes toward homosexuality which cannot be assumed to be the same as in the Philippines. Within the U.S. gay community, he has to deal with attitudes of mainstream gays toward gay minorities. In short, he has to deal with the anxieties of being a minority within a minority. He has to cope with the loneliness of someone twice removed from the mainstream of American life.

Attitudes toward homosexuality in the Filipino-American community can be glimpsed from articles and interviews with westernized gays in the popular media. The literature of gay men has also provided testimony to their experiences in America. (For this, see Manalansan, 1993). Articles about AIDS in the Filipino-American community are particularly instructive. For example, De Guzman (1989b) explains that the lack of awareness about AIDS among

Filipino-Americans is related to their view of homosexuality. Although they may openly joke about it, they find it difficult to confront the issue of homosexuality because it is a taboo subject. For Filipinos, to talk about sexuality violates the rigid conception of good taste and acceptable behavior. Aside from being a taboo subject, De Guzman (1989b, p. 12) explains that "homosexuality is still stigmatized in the community. Filipino gays and lesbians are talked about in hushed tones and families do not talk about their own homosexual relatives. This homophobia adds terror to the lives of gay Filipinos infected with AIDS as their disease hastens the exposure of their lifestyle."

The extent of homophobia in the Filipino-American community is not known. However, the possibility of widespread negative attitudes marks a shift from what is considered as generally tolerant attitudes in the Philippines and begs for an explanation. Does immigration or being in the United States change attitudes toward homosexuality? Does immigration change perception and attitudes toward other forms of deviant behavior as well?

It could be argued that negative attitudes are prevalent in some sectors of the community but not in others. Negative attitudes may be more prevalent among Filipino-Americans who have strong Catholic beliefs or among those who hold conservative social attitudes. For example, an American-born Filipino gay man acknowledged that the difficulty of disclosing to his parent that he has AIDS springs from "all sorts of cultural and religious beliefs. . . . As a Filipino, being gay is hard enough. What more if other people, especially Filipinos, find out I'm infected with AIDS?" (Pimentel, 1990).

Attitudes may also be a function of education and degree of acculturation. Filipino-Americans who are more educated and acculturated to American mainstream culture may have more liberal attitudes toward homosexuality. Shame is probably the reason why some Filipino-Americans hesitate to deal with homosexuality. Family reputation is a very strong trait among Filipinos and Filipino-Americans. In the United States, where masculinity is given a high premium, to admit having a gay son or a relative may diminish one's family honor.

Individual stories provide an idea of how attitudes of Filipino-Americans toward homosexuality may vary. Acceptance of their sexual orientation from parents and friends is an issue which most gay men have to confront in their lives. A young Filipino-American, writing about his coming-out, noted that he felt apprehensive about admitting he was gay to his parents. Like most Asians, he felt the pressure to get married and to raise a family. Nevertheless, during Thanksgiving dinner, when asked about dating and girl-friends, he informed his family that he was gay. His mother responded: "Well, . . . uh . . . Ray, I know this cute man at work. I think you'd be a perfect match." A few years later, he asked his brother about what he thought of his homosexuality. The brother replied, "Dude, I don't care if you're gay or not. You're my brother and I love you. I'll have mom's ten grandchildren" (Orquiola, 1992).

These accepting attitudes contrast sharply with the story of a thirty-two year old man who left Stockton, a farming community in San Joaquin Valley, California. In a published interview, he said:

> I needed to get in touch with my own sexuality. It was very difficult to be openly gay in a rural community. A gay person could actually put his life in jeopardy if he comes out in a very conservative setting. I was 17 years old when I was thrown out by my parents when they found out I was gay. They were quite disappointed that their youngest son who was able to finish college did not come up to their expectations. I was estranged from my parents for about four years. . . . Before I was diagnosed with ARC two years ago, my family had already accepted me back because they missed me. However, they preferred that we not talk about my being gay. (De Guzman, 1989a)

Filipinos and the American Gay Community

Being a minority within a minority, do Filipino gay men view themselves as part of a larger society? Do they feel part of the mainstream gay community or do they feel more comfortable in their own Filipino-American community? Research has yet to provide answers to these questions, although an exploratory study on

Asian-American gays and lesbians may provide a clue (Chan, 1989). A convenience sample of thirty-five men and women responded to a questionnaire dealing with issues of community affiliation, "coming-out," identity, and discrimination. When asked "In which community do you feel more comfortable?" twenty respondents chose lesbian/gay community, ten chose Asian-American, and five chose neither or both. When asked "What do you consider to be your identity?" twenty chose Asian-American lesbian woman or gay man, nine chose lesbian or gay Asian-American, and seven responded neither or both. When asked if they "feel acknowledged and accepted in lesbian/gay community?" only four responded "yes," while thirty responded "no," and one responded "unsure."

The study suggests that, at least for this sample, the lesbian/gay community is the primary reference point of identification for Asian-American lesbians and gay men. They feel more comfortable with the lesbian and gay community than with their own ethnic group. However, even if a majority in the sample identified themselves primarily as lesbian or gay, most of them feel that they are not acknowledged by the lesbian and gay community. According to Chan (1989), it suggests that "Asian-American lesbians and gay men, like other ethnic minority lesbians and gay men, find themselves in the position of not feeling totally comfortable in either community, because part of their identity is not being acknowledged." The Asian-American community may fail to see their sexual identity, while the lesbian and gay community may ignore their Asian-American identity. With respect to their experience of discrimination, a majority of gay Asian men reported that they "felt more frequently discriminated against because they were gay than because they were Asian." However, the majority of women "felt that they had experienced more discrimination because they were Asian than because they were lesbians."

IMPLICATIONS FOR SOCIAL SERVICES

An understanding of the gay Filipino in the United States must begin with an understanding of his culture and history. It cannot be denied that an individual has unique circumstances which shape his perception and understanding of the world. Yet again, the way we organize our perception of the world is rooted in our group experiences and social relations which belong to the domains of history and culture. Thus, the realities confronting the Filipino as an individual and as a member of a larger group are germane to any type of health, mental health, and social-support services in or out of the Filipino or the Asian Pacific Islander community.

Showing sensitivity starts with very practical concerns from the time a Filipino enters a clinic or meets a provider. Practitioners must be able to understand Filipino men by starting with assessment of their level of acculturation, their urban or rural residence, their family, their education, their socio-economic status, and other relevant social factors. Although they may share a common history and culture, one cannot assume that all homosexually active Filipino men are alike or that they have the same concerns or interests. As mentioned before, Filipinos differ in many social and economic characteristics. Hence, their needs and individual response to stresses may vary as well. Social workers and other service providers must be able to understand their culture without de-emphasizing their individuality. It is a common shortcoming of the dominant culture to view the colonized as an undifferentiated, homogeneous mass without regard for individual differences (Memmi, 1967). Although it cannot be denied that culture shapes personality, social service providers must distinguish between problems which are related to culture and those which are related to individual personality.

To achieve better rapport, social service workers must have a sense of the unique confluence of history and culture in an individual client. They should try to view a Filipino gay client on his own terms. Assessment might focus on identifying the cultural, social, and economic bases of personal conflict including stress in everyday life and in relationships. For Filipinos, this is likely to arise over the contradiction between homosexuality as behavior and identity. For adult immigrants–those raised in the Philippines–this may present an unanticipated set of definitions and expectations. Social service workers are likely to see three possible responses. First, adult immigrants may respond by seeking an exclusively immigrant social network as a way of staying as close to Filipino culture as possible. For instance, the switching between active and passive roles which is common in gay relations in the United States might be threatening to a Filipino *bakla*. He might search in vain for "straight men" who meet his idea of a sex partner. The probability of finding such a partner may be easier within the Filipino community which understands his way of thinking but might be more difficult in the gay mainstream community.

Second, for those who are more accepting or flexible, or who are able to accommodate to North American expectations, the response may be to socialize in the mainstream gay community. For example, a man who thought of himself as masculine or dominant might begin to think of himself as gay and explore other ways of fulfilling his sexual needs.

A third possible response may be to enter into relationships that do not threaten one's personal identity. A Filipino man who considered himself masculine might only pair with passive American sex partners who make no demands that he alter his sexual behavior.

For adult immigrants as well as for those born or raised in the United States, stress may come from the perception of not being accepted by either the Filipino community or the gay community. With respect to the Filipino community, the stigma attached to homosexuality can trigger a host of emotional problems in Filipino gay men. They may find it difficult to be taken seriously or be accorded respect because of their sexual identity. Within the gay community, they may experience discrimination because of their ethnicity. Effeminate Filipino men might be considered undesirable since North American gay men tend to prefer men who look straight. Hence, discrimination against Filipino gay men may be due to ethnicity and self-presentation. It cannot be denied, though, that the wide variety of "types" available to gay men in the United States may prove to be positive to homosexually active Filipino men as long as they find their match.

However, the impact of racism and homophobia cannot be ignored. They are destructive to self-esteem and may lead to even more problematic behavior. A typical response to both racism and homophobia is for a gay man to hate himself and, therefore, his cultural identity. He may want to change his color, his accent, his manners, and his looks in the hope that he may be acceptable to men he desires. He may cut off all connections with his family. He may withdraw from friends and his community for they remind him of the status from which he tries to break away. The hatred he has toward himself becomes manifested in his attitude toward other gays in his community or to other minorities. He begins to view them with disgust and condescencion. He develops what Rimonte (1989) calls an "attitude of contempt." If he is ever successful in breaking away from his culture, he begins to feel superior. He asks why others cannot be more like him. Social service providers must openly discuss the issue of racism and homophobia with their clients, since there is no doubt that they make life very stressful for gay minorities. It is important that clients be counseled on how to deal effectively with these issues in order to prevent further psycho-social problems.

Providers, however, must not assume that racism and homophobia uniformly affect Filipino gay men. It is wrong to assume that racism and homophobia make all Filipino gay men psychologically worse than others since their responses may vary. Some may simply ignore these issues. They may go about their everyday life feeling neither discomfort nor desire to do something about them. After all, one could argue that racism and homophobia reside in the perpetrator, not in the victim. It is ironic that victims of racism and homophobia are viewed as psychologically worse than others. They are encouraged to seek professional help while racists and homophobes are not. On the other hand, some men who recognize racism and homophobia may be able to cope effectively with the help of family and friends. Others may seek professional help while others may join groups to educate themselves and to empower their community.

CONCLUSION

Filipino homosexually active men represent a unique confluence of history and culture. Social service providers must consider the contradictions in Filipino psyche and the anxieties they may produce. Social service providers must also pay attention to sources of internal conflict, whether they are cultural, social, or economic. At the same time, they should be cognizant of individual differences among Filipino men. They should be careful not to attribute all psycho-social problems to culture. They must also address, in counselling and therapy, the issues of racism and homophobia.

REFERENCES

Agoncillo, T. A., & Guerrero, M. C. (1982). *History of the Filipino people.* Quezon City, Philippines: R. P. Garcia Publishing Co.

Blair, E. H., & Robertson, J. A. (1903). *The Philippine Islands, 1493-1803. 7* (194). Cleveland: Arthur H. Clark Co.

Blair, E. H., & Robertson, J. A. (1904). *The Philippine Islands, 1493-1803. 12* (169-321). Cleveland: Arthur H. Clark Co.

Chan, C. S. (1989). Issues of identity development among Asian-American lesbians and gay men. *Journal of Counselling and Development, 68* (1), 16-20.

De Guzman, M. (1989a). "I'm very hopeful, I'm not ready to die." *Katipunan, 2* (12), 11-12.

De Guzman, M. (1989b). AIDS among U.S. Pinoys. *Katipunan, 2* (12), 11-12.

De Guzman, M. (1992, August 4). From fashion queen to angel of mercy. *Filipinas,* pp. 47-49.

Enriquez, V. G., Herrera, S., & Tubayan, E. (1991). *Ang sikolohiyang malaya sa panahon ng krisis.* Quezon City, Philippines: Sikolohiyang Pilipino Publishing House.

Enriquez, V. G. (1993). *From colonial to liberation psychology: The Philippine experience.* Quezon City, Philippines: University of the Philippines Press.

Enriquez, V. G. (1994). *Pagbabangong-dangal: Indigenous psychology and cultural empowerment.* Quezon City, Philippines: Akademya ng Kultura at Sikolohiyang Pilipino.

Greenberg, D. F. (1988). *The construction of homosexuality.* Chicago, Il: The University of Chicago Press.

Guerrero, A. (1971). *Philippine society and revolution.* Hong Kong: Ta Kung Pao.

Hamilton-Paterson, J. (1987). *Playing with water.* New York: New Amsterdam.

Hart, D. V. (1968). Homosexuality and transvestism in the Philippines: the Cebuan Filipino bayot and lakin-on. *Behavioral Science Notes, 3* (4), 211-248.

Itiel, J. (1989). *Philippine diary: A gay guide to the Philippines.* San Francisco, CA: International Wavelength, Inc.

Manalansan IV, M. F. (1990). Tolerance or struggle: male homosexuality in the Philippines today. Paper presented at the 1990 American Anthropological Association Annual Meetings. New Orleans, LA.

Manalansan IV, M. F. (1993). (Re)locating the gay Filipino: resistance, post-colonialism, and identity. *Journal of Homosexuality, 26,* (213), 53-73.

Mathews, P. W. (1987a). *Male prostitution: Two monographs.* Sydney, Australia: Australian Book Company and Distributors.

Mathews, P. W. (1987b). Some preliminary observations of male prostitution in Manilia. *Philippine Sociological Review, 35* (3-4), 54-74.

Memmi, A. (1967). *The colonizer and the colonized.* Boston, MA: Beacon Press.

Murray, S. O. (1984). *Social theory, homosexual realities.* New York, NY: Gau-NY.

Murray, S. O. (1992). Early reports of Cebuano, Tinguian, and Sambal *Berdache.* In S. O. Murray (Ed.), *Oceanic homosexualities* (pp. 185-192). New York: Garland Publishing.

Nery, L. C. (1979). The covert subculture of male homosexual prostitutes in Metro-Manila. *Philippine Journal of Psychology, 12* (1), 27-34.

Orquiola, R. (1992, August 4). Mom, pass the turkey . . . I'm gay! *Filipinas,* pp. 56-57.

Pimentel Jr., B. (1990). AIDS and Pinoys: Silence equals death. *Katipunan, 4* (3), 13.

Reid, A. (1988). *Southeast Asia in the age of commerce, 1450-1680: The land below the seas, vol. 1.* New Haven, CT: Yale University Press.

Rimonte, N. (1989, June 1-15). Wounded by civilization. *Philippine American News,* p. 24.

Rosca, N. (1987). *Endgame.* New York: Franklin Watts.

Silva, J. (1992, August 4). Filipinos and AIDS: The unspoken crisis. *Filipinas,* p. 38-41.

U.S. Bureau of the Census. (1993). *Statistical Abstract of the United States.* Washington, D.C.: Department of Commerce.

Whitam, F. L. (1992). Bayot and callboy: Homosexual-heterosexual relations in the Philippines. In S. O. Murray (Ed.), *Oceanic homosexualities.* New York: Garland Publishing.

Whitam, F. L., & Mathy, R. M. (1986). *Male homosexuality in four societies: Brazil, Guatemala, the Philippines and the United States.* New York, NY: Praeger.

A Korean Gay Man in the United States: Toward a Cultural Context for Social Service Practice

Sue Sohng
Larry D. Icard

SUMMARY. An increasing number of Koreans are immigrating to the U.S. Little information exists for human service professionals to draw from to help Korean gay men adjust to living in America. This discussion provides a historical overview of homosexuality in Korea with insights into contemporary Korean culture. An interview with a young Korean gay man living in the U.S. illustrates the concerns and problems these men experience as they struggle to adapt to gay life in this country. Racism from the gay community and alienation from the Korean American community are salient characteristics of the problems experienced by Korean gay immigrants. To better serve the needs of these men, helping professionals must develop relationships based on trust and friendship, understand Korean attitudes toward homosexuality, and be knowledgeable of how Confucian gender ideology influences same sex relationships involving Korean gay men living in this country. *[Article copies available from The Haworth Document Delivery Service: 1-800-342-9678. E-mail address: getinfo@haworth.com]*

Sue Sohng, PhD, is Assistant Professor, University of Washington, School of Social Work, 4101 15th Avenue NE, JH-30, Seattle, WA 98195. Larry D. Icard, PhD, is Associate Professor, University of Washington, School of Social Work, 4101 15th Avenue NE, JH-30, Seattle, WA 98195.

[Haworth co-indexing entry note]: "A Korean Gay Man in the United States: Toward a Cultural Context for Social Service Practice." Sohng, Sue and Larry D. Icard. Co-published simultaneously in *Journal of Gay & Lesbian Social Services* (The Haworth Press, Inc.) Vol. 5, No. 2/3, 1996, pp. 115-137; and: *Men of Color: A Context for Service to Homosexually Active Men* (ed: John F. Longres) The Haworth Press, Inc., 1996, pp. 115-137; and: *Men of Color: A Context for Service to Homosexually Active Men* (ed: John F. Longres) Harrington Park Press, an imprint of The Haworth Press, Inc., 1996, pp. 115-137. Single or multiple copies of this article are available from The Haworth Document Delivery Service [1-800-342-9678, 9:00 a.m. - 5:00 p.m. (EST). E-mail address: getinfo@haworth.com].

115

INTRODUCTION

The United States has historically served as a refuge for immigrants seeking to escape problems in their homeland. For many homosexuals, immigrating to progressive cities in the U.S. is a welcome relief from the sexual oppression they experience in their own countries. In 1990, 798,849 Koreans were reported living in the United States (U. S. Bureau of Census, 1992). This statistic indicates that the number of Koreans in the United States has increased more than tenfold in twenty years. This statistic also suggests that social service workers will increasingly be called upon to meet the needs of Korean immigrants, including homosexual Koreans, as they strive to adapt to life in America.

Although a significant amount of information exists on the sociocultural adaptations of Korean immigrants in the U.S. (Braus, 1993; Kwang & Won, 1993; Kwang, Hursh & Shin, 1993; Nah, 1993), no attention has been given to Korean homosexuals. This article addresses this gap by providing information to aid social workers in their efforts to serve homosexual Koreans, specifically Korean gay male immigrants. In the first section we provide a historical overview of male homosexual traditions in Korea. Next, we discuss contemporary Korean culture and its significance for understanding Korean gay men. We then summarize an interview with a young Korean man that illustrates the concerns these men bring to social workers. We conclude with recommendations for social service professionals.

HISTORICAL BACKGROUND

Homosexuality in Korea has been virtually ignored by both Korean and American scholars. Homosexuality, like other forms of sexuality, is a taboo issue in Korea. This contrasts sharply with the enormous amount of literature on homosexuality from other cultures such as Greece and Japan. Although most contemporary Koreans conform to a narrowly prescribed family-based sexuality, we find a tolerance toward homosexuality in earlier periods of Korean history.

One of the earliest records in connection with homosexuality in Korea is the Hwarang of Silla in ancient Korea (Choi, K. S., 1990; Mishina, 1943; Ji, 1992; Reischauer & Fairbank, 1960). The Hwarang was founded around A.D. 576 as a strategy for recruiting handsome youth to the royal court. While singing, dancing and morally encouraging one another, they gathered flowers from the hills and mountains. They were then assembled and arranged in cosmetics and fine clothes so that royal ministers, after observing their behaviors, could select the "good ones" for the court. The Hwarang Institute encouraged filial and fraternal piety, loyalty and sincerity. Ministers and loyal subjects arose from among Hwarang, and many developed into great generals and brave soldiers.

Official histories of the Koryo Dynasty (918-1392) also contained several references to homosexual conduct among the ruling class. Seong (1989) in an historical analysis of *Halim Pylkok* noted that homosexual practices were common among ruling classes, like King Mokchong (997-1009), King Chungsun (1275-1325) and King Kongmin (1352-1374). King Chungsun maintained a long-term relationship with a male "favorite" named *Wonchung* and lavished him with a high office and title. King Kongmin was a scholar, painter and calligrapher who, toward the end of his life, appointed handsome boys called *chajewhi* (i.e., sons and brothers corps) who resided in his royal household.

After the fall of the Koryo dynasty, the Chosun dynasty (1392-1910) ushered in a shift in social, political, and moral ideology, a shift with a negative impact on homosexuality and other forms of sensuality. In order to crush the power of Buddhists, the rulers of the Chosun dynasty adopted Confucianism, in the form now referred to as Neo-Confucianism, as the governing ideal (Hahm, 1986; Lee, 1986). They expelled the previously powerful Buddhist elites and consolidated their political power based on Confucian ideology. Although other religious and ideological influences like shamanism and Taoism continued, Confucianism became the only publicly recognized ideology throughout the dynasty. Many Buddhist temples continued to exist, but by the 16th century their influence had largely waned and Neo-Confucianism came to predominate in the intellectual and spiritual life of Korea.

In contrast to the Koryo dynasty's view, which tended to be more conducive to individual gratification (Huh, 1981), the neo-Confucian doctrine stressed familial duty, moral asceticism, and moderation of feelings. With the rising Neo-Confucian views, much of the historical records on homosexual practices shifted from descriptions of the ruling elites to descriptions of commoners and lower classes. Despite official disapproval, historical accounts attest that homosexual conduct was well known in rural society during this conservative period. For instance, *Namsadang* was a troupe of male singers and actors who performed traditional puppet plays and religious and shamanist ceremonies in the countryside (Michina, 1943; Shim, 1985). These young men had a specific role as dancers but they also earned money as male prostitutes. *Namsadang* formed as "husband-and-wife" teams, traveling around the country from the middle of the Chosun dynasty onwards (Shim, 1985).

GENDER IDEOLOGY

Understanding homosexuality in contemporary Korea also requires an examination of Confucian gender ideology. Neo-Confucianism, as it has survived the westernization that has occurred during the 20th century, continues to be the most persistent, persuasive and influential ideology in East Asian history (Hsu, 1986; Lee, 1986; Kuo, 1986). It has provided Korean people with their ethical and moral norms as well as suggested methods of government (Hahm, 1986).

Three features of the Confucian gender ideology are particularly relevant for understanding same sex relationships in modern Korean society. They are: (1) gender hierarchy, (2) gender role specialization, and (3) gender segregation. The Confucian gender ideology emphasizes the roles and statuses of men and women as an integral part of the overall social order which in turn is embedded in the *Um-yang* (Chinese *yin-yang*) view of the universe. *Um* is associated with quiescence, darkness, softness, the Earth, and all that is feminine. *Yang* is associated with activity, brightness, hardness, Heaven and all that is masculine. Traditionally everything in the universe was accounted for in terms of the interaction of *um* and *yang*, and the derivation of specialized gender roles for man and woman in these terms was considered to reflect the fundamental nature of the universe. In one sense, *um* and *yang* are perfectly equal and complementary; neither *um* alone nor *yang* alone is complete. Each gives rise to the other, and their roles, though different, are strictly interdependent; together they form a single, complex unity (Tu, 1986).

In the description of the roles, however, the priority of *yang* is beyond question. With the kinship family as the fundamental social force, man is placed above woman. Men occupy the predominant position in Korean society, and are less restricted in their freedom of movement. Women on the other hand are subordinate to men and must follow them as Earth follows Heaven. This gender hierarchy produces women who follow the three obediences (obedience to father, obedience to husband when married, and obedience to sons when widowed).

In the Confucian framework, the male sphere is public, outside, and front stage, apart from the female role sphere which is domestic, inside, and backstage. For instance, a traditional Korean house usually has two separate buildings, one in the front of the property occupied by the male family head, and the other in the back for the female family members. The sex role segregation is so complete that men and women enjoy considerable autonomy in their own sphere of activity. This spatial segregation also imposes emotional distancing between men and women. Korean men and women are segregated at a young age, and the gender distinctions go beyond roles to all forms of social interaction. Men socialize primarily with men and women primarily with women.

Today, coeducation, Western ideas of romantic love, and the growing practice of dating are having an impact on the younger generation (Choi, J. S., 1982). Nevertheless, social interaction continues to take place in largely same sex, gender segregated groups. Men frequently dine and drink together after work. On weekends or holidays groups of spirited women going off on excursions are common. The impression one gets is of two societies, the world of men and the world of women, each one distinct and self-sufficient.

The relative segregation of men and women is reflected in marital norms which are quite different from those in contemporary United States. Camaraderie between men and women is given greater importance among North Americans and an intimate relationship between husband and wife is one of the primary goals of marriage. In Korean society such intimacy may or may not be part of a marriage. Marriage is principally considered as bonding of two lineage groups, not a dyadic union of man and woman as sexual partners. Being essentially a kinship matter, Korean marriages are often subservient to kin interests, such as the demand for filial piety to parents and parents-in-law (Choi, J. S., 1982; Choi, S. D., 1978; Lee, 1975). Although norms are changing, intimate love and communication between husband and wife still remain uncommon in most Korean marriages. Same sex friendships are still considered the natural place for deep and satisfying interpersonal relationships.

Consequently, friendship between members of the same sex is more developed and cultivated in Korean society than it is in the United States where the tendency is to look to marriage or its equivalent for the closest and most intimate personal relationships. What an American means by "friend" is frequently something quite casual, and friendships form and dissolve easily. Korean friendships tend to form more slowly and once formed tend to be deep and lasting, the presumption being that friends are friends for life. In Korea, mutual sharing between friends is taken for granted, and much more may be asked of a friend than is common in America.

THE OPPRESSION OF HOMOSEXUALITY IN KOREA

What does it mean to be a gay man in Korea? Why can't a man be very comfortable as a gay person in Korea when there is not as much rigidity, compared to the United States, around same-sex relationships? To answer these questions requires an understanding of kinship and family relations in contemporary Korean society. Confucianism specifies that a man cannot attain public virtue unless he internalizes domestic virtue first: a man can be a true public leader only after he cultivates himself and regulates his family in harmony (Hahm, 1986). In western societies, as urbanization and industrialization accelerate, social organization gradually aligns according to occupation and social class rather than kinship. Korea, like China and Japan, has maintained kinship as the fundamental social force to the present day (Hahm, 1986; Hahn, 1989; Lee, 1986; Tu, 1986).

Family in Korea possesses a much wider significance than that possessed by the extended family of the West. A man with affectionate family ties is given the recognition of a decent human being. Without a family a man is almost considered "non-human" (Hahm, 1986).

As such, Korean norms on kinship prevented, and still prevent, the emergence of a self-identified homosexual lifestyle independent of marriage. Koreans generally disparage homosexuality not for religious and ethical reasons, but because it disrupts the kinship tradition. An emphasis on duty, obligation, and family over personal priorities and preferences is an integral part of Confucianism. Confucianism has never approved of homosexuality. And yet, it does not condemn homosexuality as a sin or crime deserving of eternal damnation which is the case in the West (Hahm, 1986; Hinsch, 1990).

A NARRATIVE: HAN SUNG ME

It is the overwhelming importance of family and kinship that engenders much of gay oppression in Korean American communities. The following interview reveals problems commonly experienced by Korean gay men who immigrate to the United States. The interview is between one of the authors and a young Korean man in his early thirties, Han Sung Me (a fictional name).

The narrative method was used to uncover Han's experiences. The narrative uses the interview as a learner's dialogue, that is, as a relatively unstructured mutual give and take between interviewer and respondent. In this way it avoids the rigid, one way, structured interviews common in social science research. This interviewing strategy is grounded in the belief that the social work researcher is a messenger who gives voice to those who have suffered oppression. Gorman (1993) argues that social work researchers have the ability to uncover the "intensely personal, highly emotional, often brutal stories of everyday life as lived by clients and witnessed by practitioners" (p. 247). Furthermore, the narrative method of inquiry is compatible with social work values in that it encourages an exploration of a unique, client centered perspective (Goldstein, 1986; Gorman, 1993; Lincoln & Guba, 1985; Rosenau, 1992; Swigonski, 1993).

In keeping with the narrative approach, Han received a list of general questions prior to the interview. The interview covered five basic areas: (1) Korean attitudes and values on homosexuality; (2) Korean cultural values on male gender roles that affect Korean male same sex relationships; (3) the concerns of immigrant Korean gay men in adapting to gay culture in the United States; (4) support systems and self-help groups that are available to Korean gay men in the U. S., and (5) the requirements of social workers to better serve the needs of Korean gay men.

The interview itself was recorded with an audiotape and transcribed with little editing. Han reviewed the transcription for its accuracy and gave permission for the interview to be published.

The following background information sets the context for the interview. Han immigrated to the United States in his mid-twenties and enrolled in an MBA program at a small college on the west coast. He completed his degree two years before the interview and was living in a large west coast city where he was involved in a relationship with an older Caucasian man. He reported that he returned to Korea after receiving his degree and was employed by a prominent Korean company where he received a substantial salary.

However, feeling oppressed in Korea as a gay man, he reported that he resigned from his position and returned to the U.S. in hopes of living in a country more tolerant of homosexuality. He further revealed how he felt defeated in this country from the sexual racism he experienced in the gay community and the ethnic racism he experienced in the broader society. Han expressed frustration over not being able to find employment since he returned to the States two years ago. He believed racial discrimination had restricted his employment opportunities. He indicated that he felt trapped. He believed he could not get help finding employment through the Korean American community because he would be questioned on not being married. Han stated that if he turned to the Korean American community for help he would be pressured to get married. His relationship was strained not only by his inability to find employment but also by the fact that his lover's occupation required his lover to be out of the country for extended periods.

Han returned to Korea sometime after the interview. The move was unexpected and the reasons for it are unclear. The authors learned however that he plans to live in Korea and not return to the United States.

ON KOREAN ATTITUDES ABOUT HOMOSEXUALITY

Interviewer (INT)
> Let's begin by talking about Korean culture and homosexuality.

Han (HSM)
> I don't think there are any positive attitudes that Koreans hold toward homosexuality. Not because they are so negative, but because I think they have no experience whatsoever.

INT It is my understanding that certain things are considered taboo and certain things are considered ok for a Korean man in having a relationship with another man.

HSM Some of the beliefs are influenced by Confucianism. There are five different philosophies; one of them is that when you make a friend you have to trust your friend completely. You share everything with him. This philosophy created the male/male bond society in Korea. Once you get to know him, you almost share everything with another man. Korea is still a male dominated society, so most men do not make friends with a woman. Even a few years ago you would not see a man having a female friend. If you say that you have a friend it is assumed that the friend is male. This is changing little by little today.

INT Do western television programs or western movies depicting homosexuality that are shown in Korea have any influence on changing Koreans' attitudes on homosexuality?

HSM I was so surprised to hear that *The Wedding Banquet* will be playing in Korea. Obviously this movie is coming for the straight people, but the movie has many gay themes which deal with the relationship between a Caucasian and Korean male. I think it would be good to ask people about their impressions of this movie and of a [sexual] relationship between two fine men. It has been a while since I lived in Korea. When I lived in Korea they knew about homosexuality and they hear that two men sleep together and have sex together but they just don't talk about it but they ignore it.

INT So they know about it but they don't discuss it; is this just homosexuality, or is it correct to say that Koreans don't discuss their personal lives?

HSM In Korea, friends talk about everything and share almost all of their private lives. But, somehow people get so ashamed of being homosexual. For example, in my case I know some straight people who went to high school and college with me but I never felt comfortable about sharing my sex life with them. Because they have no experience and don't know anything about it, they have no basis for understanding a gay lifestyle. If they see an article that tells of one man sleeping [having sex] with another they say, "Oh, they are homo!" Homo has a very derogatory meaning in Korean; it is not very positive at all.

MALE FRIENDSHIPS AND HOMOSEXUALITY IN KOREA

INT Describe some of the Korean gender role expectations that govern male same sex relationships.

HSM Koreans never talk about homosexuality. They think of a [homosexual] person as someone who dresses in woman's clothing. They never think that a normal looking guy can be a homosexual.

   Korean culture is very family and group oriented society. I don't go out by myself here [in the U.S.] because I am so used to going out with my friends. Sometimes we even sleep together because we are good friends. This is acceptable.

INT After a certain age, does this become unacceptable?

HSM   No. For instance, here's an example. You are married and I
       am your best friend, and when I come to your place to visit
       you sleep with me and not with your wife, because your
       wife goes to bed early and we talk about our friendship and
       politics and stories and sometimes we end up sleeping in the
       same room. So with this kind of cultural background it is
       hard to describe Korean culture and values toward homo-
       sexuality.

INT   Then if there is more acceptance in Korea of men being
       together than in American society, is there a lot more flexi-
       bility in Korea on male/male relationship?

HSM   Exactly!

INT   Where is the line drawn–when does homosexual behavior
       become unacceptable?

HSM   After people find out, they just set back and say, "Oh, oh, I
       don't want to be around that guy." Somehow, they become
       very afraid of being around that person.

INT   What are they afraid of?

HSM   I don't know exactly . . . because our culture stems from
       Confucianism . . . because after you reach a certain age you
       are supposed to go out with a girl, get married and have a
       family. Perhaps they think of homosexuality as being abnor-
       mal or an unacceptable lifestyle.

INT   In this country when someone knows a person is gay some
       people don't want to be around that person because they
       don't want others to think that they are gay. Do you think
       such attitudes exist in Korea?

HSM   That may be part of it, but not as much as it is here in the
       U.S. Everything in Korea is so new, such as coming out.
       Koreans think that it is morally wrong to have sex with
       another man. Also, Korea is one of the most developed
       countries in terms of Christianity. So, most churches in
       Korea teach people that homosexuality is against God.

INT   Could you talk more about Confucianism?

HSM   It doesn't talk about homosexuality; it never talked about it. In olden days Korean people who came from poor families could not afford to get a wife even. So they would go to work for the rich people and would have to all sleep together in the same room. Also in the olden days in Korea you were not supposed to spend much time with your wife. In the village there was a social place for males to go in the winter time. In the summer time men worked so much in the fields. In the winter time, after the weather got so cold, they had nothing to do. So what do they do? They get together, all the men would get together in the same room and they would play cards, play chess, and sleep together in the same room. In those days being affectionate toward your wife was shameful. Even now a days, Koreans never kiss their wives in public. Everything has to be in the dark.

INT   Why can't a man be very comfortable as a gay person in Korea when there is not as much rigidity in that country around male roles as there is in the U.S.?

HSM   What do you mean? There is tremendous pressure! They [Korean gays] have to hide everything. People will not get suspicious of two men going to movies together, or going out to eat together. But you have to hide your feelings even though you invite your lover to your place. For example, I know of a friend who goes over to his boyfriend's place and they sleep [have sex] together and his boyfriend's wife sleeps alone but they feel awful because they have to hide everything.
        Korean gay men don't have much freedom. If they want to go on a trip for several days, they cannot do that. It used to be easier to go on a trip with another man but today the world is getting smaller and smaller. The wife questions the meaning of a real family. What is the family value? So wives are beginning to request more of their husbands.

INT   So things are beginning to change because of western culture. Western culture is having both a negative and positive influence on gay life in Korea?

HSM   Exactly! You know in Korea, once you reach a certain age you almost always have to have your own family. Once you get married people expect you to have kids; if you don't people ask what's wrong, why you don't have any children? They will ask you directly.

INT   What's an acceptable answer to that question?

HSM   There is no acceptable or right answer. I have a few close gay friends in Korea and all but one is married. They live a double life. The way my one friend could get away from all those pressures, he told his parents that he cannot function, that he is impotent. After they found out that he could not function they didn't put so much pressure on him.

INT   Currently in this country there is a lot of concern over whether openly gay men should serve in the military. How is this issue addressed in the Korean military ?

HSM   Military men must go to service for 3 or 4 years so there is a brothel around a military base. Also in Korea a lot of gay men come out through the military service because they have very good chance to sleep [have sex] with so many men who are in the same room. I did not go to the U.S. military service but in Korea we sleep on the same floor, 30 guys together and sometimes they play around. Here your culture doesn't accept that kind of behavior. There, I'm sure all straight guys know it's going on in the military. But they don't talk about it. You get vacation time only twice a year and you stay on the military base all the time so you get very horny. We sleep in the same floor or area. And some-times even the superior officer will ask a younger man to come to their corner of the floor, "you come next to my side and sleep with me." The other men know that it is happen-ing but they don't say anything about it. The guy who has pretty face like a woman is more popular. They are used. Guys who play the dominant role never see themselves as gay.

INT   What about the older Korean gay man, do you have any

insights on how the older gay man deals with his homo-sexuality?

HSM   A lot of straight people fool around with their wives but it's ok. But when these older gay people go out with another man they feel so guilty. I guess because of the social pressures, and because homosexuality is not acceptable.

In Korea it is shameful to talk about sex, but some of my friends ask me questions when I go back home. They hear that it is easy to meet men here. That's why I came to this country because here you have a lot more potential for meeting other men. There, there is nothing like that at all, no social places, no social groups, just a few gay bars.

INT   Tell me about Korean gay bars.

HSM   I get intimidated in Korea. In Korean gay bars people never talk, they never talk to strangers. I go out in Korea and if I find someone who is an attractive man, the typical way is to ask the waiter to come over. Then I pour a drink in my glass and ask the waiter to take it to that person and to tell him it is from me. Then the waiter takes the drink to the person and points out who the drink is from. That person then looks around to see who sent the drink and if he agrees or is interested in me he send another glass of beer to me. Then we look at each other and have some eye contact. Then I get more aggressive and ask the waiter if he would ask him to come over to my table or if I can come over to his table.

INT   Why do you get intimidated in Korean gay bar settings?

HSM   Because I don't like that kind of way of meeting people. Here in the U.S. it's so much easier. I can meet anybody anyway. If you see someone that you think is interesting you just go up and say hi.

INT   Do you do that?

HSM   Not much (laughs). But still other people come up to me, but there in Korea no one comes up.

CONCERNS ABOUT THE GAY COMMUNITY IN THE UNITED STATES

INT   What are some of the concerns Korean men have about the gay community in the U.S.?

HSM   First, a Korean gay must learn how to communicate and get comfortable with English. Here [in the U.S.], I try to be in good physical shape. Most gay men (in the U.S.) are so concerned with physical shape. I feel the Caucasian male is naturally in better shape. Usually the Asians have smaller bone structure. So the Asian gay male can easily be intimidated. I cannot extend my size or my shape. All I can do is go to the gym and try to stay fit. You don't see many gay men here in bad shape; once you are in bad shape here your gay life is over.
        But in Korea it is the opposite. They don't care. Each individual has his own particular taste. One of my friends likes only skin and bones. Another likes guys over 200 lbs. Here, if you are not in good shape, then it's over. Here guys go out in the winter in tight jeans and summer shirts. But in Korea, if you go out, you wear suits and ties. So many people in suits.
        Another point, I'm sure there is some racial prejudice. Maybe white men are not interested in Asian men because of their look. So I don't get aggressive enough to go over to another person to initiate a conversation because I don't want to be rejected by the other person. So, from my point of my view, these Korean people who come to the U.S. have to be more aggressive. I had to learn how to make a move. I find that even here in this city, not because they are prejudiced but because they [gay Americans] are shy people, too. Even though a person is interested in me, he doesn't come up to me and say, "Hi." I know a few Asian gay men who assume that Americans dare not be interested in them. They assume people do not come up to them because they look different. Also, they [Asian gay friends] say that only ugly, bad looking white men who have lots of money approach them. Because these men do not get the pretty white males

they go after Asian men. The older white gay men often go after Asian gay men because Asian men are a lot easier to approach, and because Asian gay men do not get much chance or opportunity to develop relationships with all those good looking white male westerners.

In our (Korean) society we always respect older people; maybe that is why many of us feel a lot more comfortable in being around older people. It seems that Koreans are much more varied in their likes for sexual partners. One of my best friends, a gay Korean male, goes for fat, old men. For him, a man has to be over 45 and has to be over 200 lbs. at least. If I say to him, "What do you think about Tom Cruise?", he would say, "He's ugly." I don't know, here American gay men are more narrow in their physical attractions. I'm sure here hundreds of thousands would say that Tom Cruise is so cute and adorable but over in Korea it is more varied. Each individual has his own taste. All my Korean gay friends, they have their own taste for what is an attractive man.

Also the Asian people physically are usually smaller, look softer, gentler, and because we are smaller, our characteristics are viewed by westerners as effeminate. Sometimes we [Korean gay men] think that in the U.S. gay community the macho guy is the most popular and desired. So sometimes I feel I am less attractive. I don't say I'm not very popular, but I know a lot of gays go for butch guys. If you see one Oriental and one Caucasian as a couple usually people stereotype the Oriental in a role like a woman, and assume that the Oriental likes the bottom and Caucasian likes the top. These stereotypes bother me.

INT.   How do you deal with that?

HSM   It's no problem. I don't care. There are some people who don't care. I always try to have a positive attitude. Also, I don't blame all those people who go for a bigger size, that's their taste. I have heard good comments about my body and its shape. I've heard some men say that they like it (my body) because my skin is so smooth and there is no hair. I have run into some westerners who say they don't like guys with a lot of (body) hair. Sometimes I ask guys who go out with me, why are you interested in me? And I've heard a lot comment, "Because most Asian men have no body hair and they have very smooth skin, I just can't stand hair, no matter how sexy a person looks."

SOCIAL SUPPORT AND SELF-HELP GROUPS

INT   Are there Korean Gay support groups or organizations?

HSM   No, the funny thing is you don't see many Korean gay men here (referring to a U.S. city). You see a lot of different ethnic backgrounds like Vietnamese, some Chinese and some Japanese. I don't know why you don't see as many Korean gay men because I am sure we have the same percentage of gay men as other races.

INT   One would think that Korean gay men are far ahead of Vietnamese gay men in adjusting to gay life in America.

HSM   No, this is not so. For example, Thailand is so far behind Korea in terms of its economy but so far ahead in terms of its acceptance of homosexuality. Thai people, Thai straight people don't care if you are gay or not. The gay industry is far better in Vietnam and the Philippines than in Korea.

INT   So among the Asian people who are gay who come to this country, who do you turn to for support?

HSM   I try to find other Korean gay males, because I get so lonesome. Sometimes I seek out other Asian gay men.

INT   Are there any national networks or organizations for Korean American men in this country?

HSM   I do not know of any national Korean gay organizations. There is a local organization called "Asian and Friends," and I've heard of another called "Westerners Who Have Asian Boyfriends."

INT   Do you know of the organization called "Men of All Colors"?

HSM   Yes, but I don't go to support groups any more because men
      go there to play games [socialize] and meet people. They
      don't do too much politically. I suggested, "You guys
      should do more than this, like have a discussion on a com-
      mon topic." But mainly they have a lot of parties and pot-
      luck dinners. A lot of the time a lot of older white men go to
      these meetings to try and pick-up Asians. I get really intimi-
      dated by a lot of older white males who come up and ask me
      to lunch. I think Korean gay people are more reserved than
      any other gay people.

RECOMMENDATIONS
FOR SOCIAL SERVICE PROVIDERS

INT   What are some suggestions or recommendations you might
      give to social workers and other human services profession-
      als who want to better serve the needs of Korean gay men?

HSM   Before you social workers do anything for him [Korean gay
      man] you have to make him feel comfortable. For instance,
      if you want to go into business with someone in Korea you
      have to make your business [client] your friend. You have to
      get to know him well. You have to give him a good impres-
      sion that you trust him, you really like him and you are
      really interested in him. You have to get close to him as a
      person.
         If he gets comfortable with you, he will expose himself
      to you. For instance, I am a businessman, so if you want to
      do business with me you must find out what I have as a
      hobby. If I like singing then you should invite me to a
      karaoke bar, even though you may not know how to sing
      you should try to sing for him. Try to get close to him first,
      not do business first. After getting familiar with a person,
      then go with the person to the bar, or to a restaurant.
         In general, Korea is a very homogenous society, so
      they tend to like their own people. Koreans don't show their
      emotions, but emotions play a very important role in what a
      person thinks. We don't show our emotions and feelings to

strangers, but once we feel comfortable with a person we try to share everything with him.

Also get to know something about a person's culture. For example, if the Korean gay man asks you if you like kim chee, you might say, "Gee, I don't know what it is." But you should not say, "No, I don't like it," because this could be offensive.

CONCLUSION AND RECOMMENDATIONS

Over the past several years there has been a steady increase in the number of Koreans immigrating to this country. Korean gay men are likely to be included among these immigrants and when they are, they expect that their lives will improve in the United States. Such expectations, however, are not always realized. As this interview suggests, at least four dilemmas confront gay Korean immigrants. First, like any immigrant they must come face to face with the problems of achieving in a competitive, free market economy. Second, they must adapt to the subculture of gay American men. Third, they must rethink their relationship with Korean Americans in the United States. Finally, for those seeking services, they must adapt to social services in the United States.

Like most Koreans, gay Koreans come to the United States in the hope of improving their economic circumstances. Han came here with the hope of obtaining an MBA and going on to a good career and comfortable life. He did complete his degree but he has yet to find his niche in the American economy. He believes that racial discrimination may be playing a part in his inability to find suitable employment. Unemployment rates are relatively low among Asian immigrants and research suggests that within fifteen years, Asian immigrants will achieve incomes as high as those of other Americans (Neidert & Farley, 1985). Nevertheless, as the case of Han shows, economic achievement is not a certainty, especially when racism may be used to block opportunities.

Gay Koreans also come to America to get away from the hostile attitudes that prevail in Korea. Although they are likely to acknowledge a number of good things about Korean gay life, especially male friendship patterns and the relative lack of concern about body image and physical fitness, a desire for greater sexual freedom motivates their move to the United States. Adaptation to the gay American subculture, however, is not always easy. Han feels a sense of inadequacy and inferiority when he compares himself to the norms used in the gay community to judge people. Although he is in a relationship with an American man, he feels that he is unattractive physically and that the kind of American men he is attracted to will not be attracted to him.

When gay Korean immigrants experience personal difficulties they are often afraid to seek help from heterosexual Koreans. Unlike their heterosexual counterparts, Korean gay men hesitate to turn to Korean services for support and help in adjusting to American life. The emphasis on kinship and the fear of being forced into an arranged marriage are two major reasons why Han was reluctant to seek support from other Koreans. This was the case for Han even though not seeking help from heterosexual Koreans may have contributed to his unfavorable economic and emotional condition. Lacking the emotional support and the potential economic contacts that Korean community services may provide leave Korean gay men in a vulnerable position.

Finally, gay Korean immigrants are also likely to have difficulties adapting to the role of client within American social services. Han was careful to point out that disclosing and sharing personal problems with a stranger, regardless of his or her professional status, is antithetical to Korean cultural expectations. He hesitated to use services in the Korean community but he also hesitated to use services in general. Han suggests that Koreans expect to unburden themselves within the context of a trusting, personal relationship.

In order to provide culturally appropriate services, American social service workers need to become familiar with Korean culture and especially Confucian gender ideology as these affect interpersonal relations. They must also understand that the ideas gay men raised in Korea have about homosexual relationships do not prepare them for adapting to the gay American community. They are likely to de-emphasize the physical aspects in favor of the more spiritual and social aspects of sexual unions. Their knowledge about life in America is likely to come from western media and may also represent both over-positive and over-negative stereotypical thinking.

Similarly, heterosexual Korean Americans who wish to serve gay Koreans will have to gain a better understanding of homosexuality, the Korean and American gay communities, and ways of supporting a healthy gay sexual identity. If they are to help gay Koreans they must understand the limitations that Confucian gender ideology imposes on them and must avoid trying to force these men to conform to historical expectations.

In order for social workers and other human service professionals to better serve the needs of gay Korean immigrants the following suggestions are offered. The first grouping focuses on general service needs while the second focuses on the delivery of direct services.

Providing General Services

- Understanding the conflict between the desire for same sex intimacy and the desire to remain connected to Korean cultural traditions is an underlying component of services.

- Efforts should be made to sensitize Korean Americans to the needs of their gay and lesbian members.

- Efforts should be made to sensitize those who work in gay (and lesbian) services about the needs of gay Korean immigrants.

- Efforts must be directed to providing outreach through services in the gay community, the Korean community, and the network of agencies in the wider community.

- Efforts are required to inform gay Korean immigrants of all the resources that are available through human service professionals and agencies.

Providing Direct Services

- Focus on developing a relationship of trust and friendship prior to initiating efforts to engage in problem-solving.

- Understand Korean values and attitudes on gender ideology, homosexuality and male friendship patterns and try to offer help in a way that enables Korean clients to remain identified with their community yet accepted as gay men.

• Be knowledgeable of how Korean normative expectations for men differ from American expectations.

In summary, Korean gays may experience problems adjusting to life in America. Gay Korean immigrants are likely to experience economic problems as well as social and sexual conflicts. Although adjustment to new circumstances is always difficult, prejudice and discrimination may make adjustment even more difficult. Gay immigrants fear the anti-homosexual prejudice of other Koreans and the anti-Korean prejudice of Americans. As Korean immigrants are often highly educated, many will make significant contributions to the United States. Social service workers should not fail to help these men fulfill their potential.

REFERENCES

Braus, P. (1993). Welcome to America, here's your phone. *American Demographics, 15*(1), 11.

Choi, Jae Suk (1982). *The study of modern family*. Seoul, Korea: Il Ji Sa.

Choi, Kwang Sik. (1990). Reexamination of Hwarang of Silla. In J. S. Choi (Ed.), *Korean society and history* (pp. 459-480). Seoul, Korea: Il Ji Sa.

Choi, Sin Duck (1978). *Marriage and family*. Seoul, Korea: Ewha Women's University Press.

Goldstein, H. (1986). Toward the integration of theory and practice: A humanistic approach. *Social Work, 31*, 352-357.

Gorman, J. (1993). Postmodernism and the conduct of inquiry in social work. *Affilia, 8*(3), 247-264.

Hahm, Pyong Choon (1986). *Korean jurisprudence, politics and culture* (pp. 291-299). Seoul, Korea: Yonsei University Press.

Hahn, Nam Jae (1989). *The study of the contemporary Korean family*. Seoul, Korea: Il Ji Sa.

Hinsch, B. (1990). *Passions of the cut sleeve: The male homosexual tradition in China*. Berkeley: University of California Press.

Hsu, F. L. (1986). Confucianism and its culturally determined manifestations. *The Psycho-cultural dynamics of the Confucian family: Past and present* (pp. 23-46). Seoul, Korea: International Cultural Society of Korea.

Huh, H. S. (1981). *The study of Koryo society*. Seoul, Korea: Asia Munwhasa.

Ji, Kyo Hyon. (1992). Reexamination of Silla Hwarang Yonku by Ayukai and Mishina. In Ji Kyun Kim (Ed.), *Silla Hwarang Yonku* (pp. 105-130). Seoul, Korea: Hankuk Jungshin Munhwa Yonkuwon.

Kuo, E. (1986). Confucianism and the family in an urban-industrial society. In W. H. Slote (Ed.), *The psycho-cultural dynamics of the Confucian family: Past and present* (pp. 113-144). Seoul, Korea: International Cultural Society of Korea.

Kwang, C. K., & Won, M. H. (1993). Beyond assimilation and pluralism: Syncretic sociocultural adaptation of Korean immigrants in the U.S. *Ethnic and Radical Studies, 16*(4), 696-715.

Kwang, C. K., Hurch, W. M., & Shin, K. (1993). Generation differences in Korean immigrants' life conditions in the United States. *Sociological Perspectives, 36*(3), 257-271.

Lee, K. (1975). *The structural analysis of Korean family.* Seoul, Korea: Il Ji Sa.

Lee, K. (1986). Confucian tradition in the contemporary Korean family. In W. H. Slote (Ed.), *The psycho-cultural dynamics of the Confucian family: Past and present* (pp. 3-18). Seoul, Korea: International Cultural Society of Korea.

Lincoln, E., & Guba, E. (1985). *Naturalistic inquiry.* Newbury Park, CA: Sage.

Mishina, S. (1943). *Chosen kodai kenkyu dai-ichibu: Shiragi karo no kenkyu.* Tokyo, Japan.

Nah, K. H. (1993). Perceived problems and service delivery for Korean immigrants. *Social Work, 38*(3), 289-297.

Neidert, L. J., & Farley, R. (1985). Assimilation in the United States: An analysis of ethnic and generation differences in status and achievement. *American Sociological Review, 50*, 840-850.

Reischauer, E., & Fairbank, J. (1960). *East Asia and great tradition.* Boston: Houghton Mifflin.

Rosenau, P. (1992). *Post-modernism and the social sciences.* Princeton, NJ: Princeton University Press.

Seong, H. G. (1989). The dating of Hallimbuolgok. *Hankuk Hakpo, 15*(3), 56-78.

Shim, W. S. (1985). *Indigenous culture and people's conscience–Minsok Munhwa and Minjung Eusik*, 225-250. Seoul, Korea: Dosue Chulpan.

Swigonski, M. (1993). Feminist standpoint theory and the questions of social work research. *Affilia, 8*(2), 171-183.

Tu, Wei-ming (1986). An inquiry on the five relationships in Confucian Humanism. In W. H. Slote (Ed.), *The Psycho-cultural dynamics of the Confucian family: Past and present* (pp. 175-196). Seoul, Korea: International Cultural Society of Korea.

U.S. Bureau of Census. (1992). Current Population Reports Series P20-459. *The Asian and Pacific Islander population in the United States.* Washington, D. C.: U. S. Department of Commerce.

An Applied Research Agenda
for Homosexually Active Men of Color

Larry D. Icard
John F. Longres
James H. Williams

SUMMARY. This paper outlines a research agenda for designing and implementing services to gay men of color. The paper reviews the anthropological, historical, and international literature on homosexuality for its implications for contemporary service delivery. The paper proposes that a problem-solving model that recognizes the central importance of empathy and rapport may be used to organize research. The paper concludes with a discussion of methodological issues. *[Article copies available from The Haworth Document Delivery Service: 1-800-342-9678. E-mail address: getinfo@haworth.com]*

As is true in any field of practice, the delivery of services to gay men of color requires good research. This paper shows that although the anthropological and historical literature provides a good backdrop, research on contemporary service issues–including needs

---

Larry D. Icard is Associate Professor, University of Washington, School of Social Work, 4101 15th Avenue NE, Seattle, WA 98195. John F. Longres is Professor, University of Washington, School of Social Work, 4101 15th Avenue, NE, Seattle, WA 98195. James H. Williams is Assistant Professor, George Warren Brown School of Social Work, Washington University, One Brookings Drive, St. Louis, MO 63130.

[Haworth co-indexing entry note]: "An Applied Research Agenda for Homosexually Active Men of Color." Icard, Larry D., John F. Longres, and James H. Williams. Co-published simultaneously in *Journal of Gay & Lesbian Social Services* (The Haworth Press, Inc.) Vol. 5, No. 2/3, 1996, pp. 139-164; and: *Men of Color: A Context for Service to Homosexually Active Men* (ed: John F. Longres) The Haworth Press, Inc., 1996, pp. 139-164; and: *Men of Color: A Context for Service to Homosexually Active Men* (ed: John F. Longres) Harrington Park Press, an imprint of The Haworth Press, Inc., 1996, pp. 139-164. Single or multiple copies of this article are available from The Haworth Document Delivery Service [1-800-342-9678, 9:00 a.m. - 5:00 p.m. (EST). E-mail address: getinfo@haworth.com].

139

and strengths, service methods, and service outcomes–is sorely needed.

Until recently the problem of effective social service delivery was focused on the question of normalcy. Whereas in the past, service providers treated homosexual conduct and identity as pathologies to be overcome, today, with some exceptions, services are more likely to affirm their normalcy. This is an important social reform but, in itself, does not assure effective service delivery. Today the problem of effective service delivery has shifted to interventions that will lead to positive outcomes with all men.

The need to provide interventions that are consonant with the ethnic and racial background of clients is increasingly recognized. The all-important process of engaging clients and offering them services they are willing to accept can be severely thwarted if service providers fail to take into account ethnic and racial stratification as well as cultural norms and expectations. Although such themes have been addressed in the general literature on social service delivery, they are only beginning to be addressed with regard to gay men of color.

This article examines the literature on male homosexual conduct and identity with an eye toward identifying research needs and questions. Our primary concern has to do with applied research, research useful in the design of policies, programs and practice strategies. With this in mind, we begin with a review of the vast contributions made by anthropologists, historians, and observers of the international gay rights movement.

This literature sets the tone for thinking about services to gay men of color in the United States today. We follow this with a discussion of a problem-solving framework that includes the important principle of taking the point of view of clients and constituents. This framework is useful for articulating three chief areas of research: research on needs and strengths; research on help-seeking, service delivery, and help acceptance; and research on the evaluation of services. Finally, we examine a number of methodological issues that must be taken into account in doing research with men of different ethnic and racial backgrounds.

THE CONTRIBUTIONS OF HISTORY
AND ANTHROPOLOGY

There is a vast literature on homosexual conduct and identity across cultures. As an indication of this, Dynes (1987) offers an annotated bibliography that includes 159 pages of entries on history, area studies, and cultural anthropology. These entries focus on anthropological studies that help us understand homosexual behavior in societies from every continent and every period of history. Similarly, Greenberg (1988) offers an exhaustive cultural and historical analysis of homosexuality that includes a discussion of homosexuality in African, Asian, Pacific Island and Native North and South American societies. Katz's (1976) *Gay American History* and Duberman's (1989) anthology, *Hidden from History,* include important material that all who work with homosexually active men of color should be familiar with.

From an applied perspective, historical and anthropological studies give answers to at least two central service issues. The first has to do with the incidence of homosexual conduct across ethnic and racial groups: "Is homosexual conduct universal?" The second has to do with whether homosexuality is understood in the same way across ethnic and racial groups: "Is homosexual identity universal?"

THE UNIVERSALITY OF HOMOSEXUAL CONDUCT

An important issue in setting up policies and programs is whether homosexual conduct is present in all ethnic and racial groups. Should social service providers expect that homosexual conduct will be present in all groups? In this regard it is not uncommon to hear minority spokespeople claim that homosexuality represents western values, capitalist depravity, or sinful, barbaric customs.

Anthropologists have long held that homosexual conduct is culturally determined. Based on the analysis of pre-industrial or kinship structured societies, they have contended that some societies show little or no incidence of homosexual conduct while others show a great deal. For instance, homosexual conduct was openly practiced in a number of early societies throughout Europe and Asia. It was also evident in a number of Native American people and among people in New Guinea and the Pacific Islands. On the other hand, homosexuality appears to be absent or rare among such kin-structured societies as the Muria of India, the Fan of Gabon or the Dani of New Guinea. It has also not been reported among the Truk, Giliyak, Sebei, Kikuyo, Comanche, Ifugao, Jivaro, Lepcha, Lesu, Mambicuara or Timbira (Greenberg, 1988). Margaret Mead (1935), who observed no homosexuality among the Arapesh and Mundugumor, offered an interesting hypothesis to explain such apparent variation. She suggested that homosexual conduct was present in societies that made sharp distinctions in the role expectations of men and women. Conversely, she asserted that homosexual conduct will not be found in societies that promote androgynous role expectations. The underlying message, however, was that homosexuality was not a universal phenomena and would disappear altogether if societies refrained from creating rigid sex-role expectations.

Although this point of view is widespread, it has been recently challenged. Greenberg (1988) argues that homosexuality was probably present in all kin-structured societies. He contends that conclusions drawn from older anthropological literature are not reliable. Most ethnographers ignored the subject and when they did discuss it, they did it largely in passing. Even when discussed at length, we cannot always have confidence in the findings. Because of the complexity of inter-society relationships, many informants may have given what they perceived as the socially desirable response to an outsider's questions. Furthermore, because sexual mores have been severely altered by the influence of missionaries, school teachers sent from abroad, and traders, government agents, tourists and even anthropologists, we cannot trust statements made after contact with the west occurred. Greenberg states:

> Over the past few centuries, much of the world has undergone a massive shift in the frequency and social acceptability of same-sex sexual relations. Information about these topics acquired after decades or centuries of contact with whites, and

after the destruction of an indigenous way of life, cannot be casually assumed to hold for the pre-contact period. (p. 80)

Homosexual conduct is probably universal. Certainly with regard to modern societies in general and American society in particular, homosexual conduct exists among all American ethnic and racial minority groups: African-, Asian and Pacific Island-, Latino-, and Native-Americans. The AIDS epidemic has made this abundantly clear. Epidemiologists have found that African- and Latino-American men are over-represented and significant numbers of Asian- and Native-American men have also been infected (Centers for Disease Control and Prevention [CDC], 1994; Easterbrook et al., 1993). Social service administrators who, like earlier anthropologists, confuse lack of acceptance with lack of existence are likely to eliminate some potentially valuable services.

THE SOCIAL CONSTRUCTION OF HOMOSEXUAL CONDUCT AND IDENTITY

There is considerable evidence that the way homosexuality is practiced and understood differs along historical and cultural lines. Services that assume that men from all groups will understand their homosexuality in the same way are likely to fail men of color.

No society gives full acceptance to all forms of sexual expression. Just as heterosexual conduct and identity are shaped by changing norms and traditions, so are homosexual conduct and identity. Norms circumscribe such things as permissible partners, permissible ways of demonstrating affection, and permissible sexual behaviors. They also help to shape the meaning individuals attach to their homosexual conduct.

In contemporary America, norms about homosexual conduct and identity are being reshaped by the Lesbian, Gay and Bisexual Movement. Two principle trends seem to stand out. In the first place, homosexual identity is determined by the sex of the chosen partner. In the second place, homosexual unions are expected to be long-term, free of expectations about roles in the sex act, and between consenting adults from the same age cohort and general social standing. Historical evidence suggests that these norms represent an emerging trend. Homosexual relations in earlier generations, for instance, gave greater emphasis to age differences and to differences in sex act expectations.

Contemporary gay-American norms may not hold among African-, Asian-, Latino- and Native-American men and the reasons may be both cultural and historical. In some groups, for instance, "a homosexual identity" has little to do with the choice of sexual partner but rather with the taking on of "non-male roles" in society as well as in the sex act. William's (1986) discussion of Native American societies, echoed in this anthology by Tafoya (this volume), shows that the *berdache* or *two-spirited people* of the past were men who cross-dressed; performed special roles in the religious, military, family, and economic life of the tribe; and generally accepted the "female role" in sexual relations with "normal men." Rodriguez (this volume) calls attention to similar norms: the Filipino *bakla* tends to identify as a woman and only have relations with "normal men." Zamora-Hernández and Patterson (this volume) indicate that the separation between sexual object and sex act behavior is an important distinction for many Latinos as well. Latino men may think of themselves as heterosexual regardless of the sex of their partner so long as they are performing what they perceive as the male sex role.

At least one other culturally-based pattern is worth noting. In many societies homosexual conduct is considered normal, even desirable, so long as it is confined to adolescence and very young adulthood (Greenberg, 1988). In adulthood these men are expected to revert completely to a family-based, heterosexual life. Such a pattern has been described among the early Greeks and Romans but for our purposes there is evidence that this pattern of homosexual conduct is found in the traditions of recent immigrants from Japan, Asia and the Pacific Islands, North Africa and the Mid-east. In this form, men who participate in sex with other men see themselves as entirely normal. They would never take on an identity as a homosexual so long as they expect to marry and procreate in a heterosexual marriage.

In summary, the historical and anthropological literature suggests that homosexual conduct is a universal phenomena. Nevertheless, we should not expect cultural norms around the expression of this conduct and especially around the idea of a homosexual identity to be universal.

THE CONTEMPORARY INTERNATIONAL LITERATURE

Culture, like any form of human social behavior, is constantly changing. In this regard, there is a good deal of literature pointing to important emerging trends in Asian, Latin American, and other nations from which the United States is presently receiving immigrants and refugees. This literature is clear in pointing out that the contemporary lesbian and gay movement is having a profound worldwide effect on homosexual conduct and identity. The gay rights movement is an international phenomenon with appeals to many different kinds of men. This has been shown in at least three of the articles in this volume. Rodriguez (this volume) acknowledges that western ideas of conduct and identity are evident side by side with the traditional *bakla* in the Philippines. Similarly, Zamora-Hernández and Patterson's article also discusses the effects of the gay rights movement in reshaping issues of sexuality among Central and South American men. One of the insights provided by Sohng and Icard's article included in this collection is that the evolving gay subculture in the United States may be a reason for immigration among men from industrializing nations.

The implications of this international literature for working with new immigrants to the United States needs to be spelled out. From an ethnic sensitive point of view, easy generalizations about cross group differences are impossible. Since the norms in their homelands are likely to be evolving, service to immigrants of color requires that we have a good sense of the extent to which individual men conform to their traditional norms or operate within a set of more western ideas. Services should probably assume that these men will be somewhere in between, neither entirely traditional nor entirely western in their ideas. Research to clarify the way immigrants and refugees understand their sexuality is therefore essential.

AN APPLIED RESEARCH AGENDA

We are concerned with promoting research that will have particular usefulness for the development of services, programs and policies. Although there is no single agreed-upon definition of social work research, the use of the problem-solving model as a framework for a research agenda holds a good deal of promise (see Figure 1). In brief, the problem-solving model posits that people identify problems, analyze their causes, make and execute plans to overcome them, and retrospectively evaluate the success of their endeavors. If they are working with professional helpers, problem-solving is believed to be greatly facilitated by an empathic relationship in which helper understands client in his or her own terms. In actuality, problem-solving is rarely a simple progression of logical and linear steps. Nevertheless, the framework serves as a useful heuristic device in practice and, we argue here, in research.

For our purposes, the problem-solving model calls attention to three overlapping research foci: the identification and analysis of needs and strengths, the planning and execution of strategies of intervention, and the evaluation of interventions. Furthermore, it suggests a fourth research focus. The problem-solving model also calls attention to the need to study issues related to the ability of helpers to understand clients as they understand themselves. Each

FIGURE 1. A Problem-Solving Framework for an Applied Research Agenda

Relationship Themes	Needs and Strengths	Service Delivery Themes	Outcome Studies
Identity	Health and mental health issues	Client help-seeking behaviors	Client satisfaction
	Basic and higher order needs and resources	Social service help-giving behaviors	Effectiveness of intervention
	Life span issues	Client help-accepting issues	

of these will be used to identify research themes that we believe will enhance service provision.

RESEARCH ON CLIENTS, CONSTITUENTS AND THEIR SYSTEMS

We take a broad definition of the term practice. Practice includes direct services to individuals, couples, families, groups and communities. Such practice incorporates working to prevent or ameliorate problems through altering or changing clients as well as altering the environments in which their problems have emerged. Practice also includes providing indirect services such as program development and policy formulation and advocacy.

In setting a research agenda, therefore, we should not narrowly focus our lens. As will be noted, we do need research on individual men but this does not mean that we should avoid research on the environments in which they live. Environments serve both to support and hinder human development. The problems and strengths of gay men of any color, therefore, cannot be understood outside of family, partners, friends, community, organizations, and indeed the society in which they live. Studies that look at the social context are as important as those that look at individual behavior.

The Point of View of Clients and Constituents

Understanding issues of identity and integration into community life are the essential starting points for building rapport with clients and constituents. Identity refers to how people understand themselves individually or collectively. For our purposes two forms of social identity stand out: how men understand their sexual urges and how men understand their attachments to society and in particular the communities of which they are a part. Community integration is the objective component of identity; it describes the groups, organizations and interpersonal networks that define the everyday experiences of individuals. Having an understanding of both of these enables service providers, community workers and planners to start where the client is. In the case of outreach services, understanding issues of identity and integration into community life enables us to devise strategies that will afford access to services by as wide a segment of the population as possible.

The historical and anthropological literature suggests that men from different societies are likely to understand homosexual conduct in different ways. For some, homosexual conduct will be considered a sin or a disease while for others it is a form of normal behavior. For some, homosexual conduct, depending on the age in which it occurs or on the role taken in the sex act, will have no implication for social identity. For others, any sexual contact with someone of the same sex will be the basis of identity.

Research on gay men of color in the contemporary United States is very much in its infancy, yet the themes of sexual conduct and identity have been central. Large scale comparative surveys between European-American and American men of color are few and far between. When they exist they are likely to compare white, black and occasionally Latino men.

Although Kinsey (1948) studied the sexual conduct, attitudes, and feelings of white and black men, these results were not published until 1979 (Gebhard & Johnson, 1979). Bell and Weinberg (1978) systematically compared black and white men on conduct, identity, attitudes, and social networks. Their data suggested relatively few statistically significant differences between white and black men. The study reported in this collection by Ryan, Longres, and Roffman also found few statistically significant differences among a non-random sample of African-American, Latino-American and European-American men in their sexual identities, attitudes about sex, and lifestyles.

The 1991 National Survey of Men also provides some interesting comparisons on the sexual behavior of black and white men (Billy, Tanfer, Grady, & Klepinger, 1993). Although the survey found that 2.4% of white men and 1.4% of black men reported same sex activity, the results are questionable. A full 13% of white men and 5% of black men indicated they had not experienced coitus in spite of acknowledging that they were cohabiting or had a regular sex partner. According to the researchers, these findings raise the possibility that the men could have been in homosexual relationships.

Finally, since the rise of the AIDS epidemic, a number of studies have repeatedly found that the incidence of bisexuality among African-American and Latino men is higher than that among European-American men (Chu, Peterman, Doll, Buehler & Curran, 1992; Karon & Berkelman, 1991). These, however, do not often go beyond the study of sexual conduct and as a result shed little light on identity and sexual attitudes.

Multiple Identities

In a multi-group society like our own, communities often compete for the allegiance of members. For our purposes, homosexually active men of color may feel the pull between allegiance to a racial and ethnic community and involvement in the gay community. There are a number of ways men of color can handle the issue of community membership. They may give total allegiance to one community, that is, they may decide that they are gay or that they are a member of an ethnic minority but not both. Conversely, they may attempt to piece together a multiple identity, one that integrates aspects of both groups.

Johnson (1982) documented the push and pull experienced by African-American men as they try to blend their sexual desires with their ethnic affiliation. He found that the men he studied were torn between their identity as an African-American, who happened to be interested in sex with men, and a gay American, who happened to be African-American. Icard (this volume) suggests that a third alternative is possible in the development of a uniquely African-American gay sub-community. That this in fact occurs can be seen in the ethnic-gay hybrid communities that have been in existence for a long time in many large American cities. Those living in New York and Los Angeles, for instance, should be well aware of organizations, gay bars, bath houses, and other community organizations that have historically catered to particular ethnic groups. Through these activities homosexually active men of color often meet and form friends with others from their same group.

The issue of multiple identities goes beyond the pull between gayness and ethnicity. In a case study by Luczak (1993), Pablo, a black, gay and deaf man talks sympathetically of his struggle for identity:

> Well, since my skin color is visible, they can identify me as black. Then they find out I'm deaf. As for being gay, it's a sticky situation. I'm not really in the closet, but I just have to use my best judgment to trust people to accept me as a gay person. (p. 39)

In summary, these studies suggest that research is needed to clarify a number of issues related to identity and community integration. We need information in the variation that exists both between and within groups in terms of their sexual conduct, sexual identity, and relative involvement in the gay and ethnic communities. At the individual level, we need to know how men struggle to put their multiple identities together. Furthermore, we need information on the attitudes and behaviors of heterosexual members of ethnic and disability communities to discern the likely support or pressure individual men may experience. Similarly, we need information on the attitudes and behaviors of white gay men with regard to gay and/or disabled men of color.

THE NEEDS AND STRENGTHS OF CLIENTS AND CONSTITUENTS

Social work practice begins with the actual or potential problems experienced by client systems. Empathic practitioners work to identify the problems for which services may be needed, analyze the bio-psycho-social factors related to them, and build on existing personal and environmental strengths to prevent or ameliorate them. What research themes will best help social services and direct service practitioners prepare for working with clients? What kinds of needs should they be ready to deal with? What are the strengths from which to build service?

Health and Mental Health Problems

A common approach to research is to determine the epidemiology of various health and mental health problems, including risk factors, likely to affect particular populations. A good deal of the recent research on men of color has focused on the incidence and prevalence of HIV disease. Given the severe effects this disease has had on men of color, the amount of money spent is justifiable. Following this logic, attention should also be given to the epidemiology of alcohol and drug use, depression, and other disorders or problems in living that affect men of color.

Although studies of specific health and mental health problems are necessary, a research agenda should not be limited to them. In the first place, they represent reactive research that leads to over-reliance on rehabilitative services. Secondly, they tend to emphasize problems and play into the idea that gay men of color have few if any strengths. We suggest therefore that a proactive approach that enables us to call attention to strengths must supplement epidemiological studies of problems and risks.

Research on Needs and Strengths

Research is required to determine the needs and strengths of homosexually active men of color. A framework based in Maslow (1954), and articulated by Hartman and Laird (1983), may prove useful. This framework identifies basic and higher order human needs and measures the resources available for meeting them. Because resources in turn may exist internally (psychological strengths) or externally (strengths through formal and informal support), a research agenda need not focus us only on the men themselves, but on the communities and neighborhoods in which they live.

With regard to men of color the distinction between basic and higher order needs cannot be overlooked. Basic needs refer to nutrition, shelter, protection, health, and communication (Hartman & Laird, 1983). In one way or another they are rooted in the material resources available to individual men and their environments. These resources include adequate and varied diet, housing, accessible medical services, safe neighborhoods, and available transportation, telephone, and postal services. Men of color–especially African, Latino and Native Americans–are disproportionately found among the undereducated, unemployed, and homeless. By extension we might assume that they will not be able to easily meet their basic needs.

Yet, we do not know whether homosexually active men are different from non-homosexually active men of color. Bell and Weinberg (1978) reported that black homosexual men were generally more educated, more likely to be in skilled occupations, and more likely to be in occupational positions of "public trust" than black heterosexual men. Furthermore, they do not report large differences between white and black homosexual men on these indexes of basic human needs. These findings may be questioned, however, since Bell and Weinberg worked from within the gay community to develop their non-random sample. It may be that gay men of color who come to the attention of researchers through the gay community represent a more middle class population. Using random sampling techniques, for instance, Harry (1990) suggests that non-white and lower educated men are more likely to affirm that they "are sexually attracted to members" of their own sex than is generally acknowledged in studies that rely on samples drawn from the gay community.

Higher order needs include belonging and feeling connected, educational and intellectual enrichment, spiritual and religious needs, the need for autonomy, and the need for generativity (Hartman & Laird, 1983). The resources necessary for meeting these cover the existence of partners, kin, and friends; good schools and available leisure time activities, opportunities to participate in religious organization; gratifying work; and opportunities for the creative exercise of physical and intellectual capacities.

Research is necessary on the ability of men of color to meet these needs. Only the needs of belongingness and connectedness appear to have been studied with any regularity. Bell and Weinberg (1978) and Ryan, Longres, and Roffman indicate that gay men of color may be as able to meet such needs as white, non-Hispanic gay men. These results, owing to the nature of their sampling, must be taken cautiously, however.

Life Cycle and Age Cohort Research

Many social services are designed around the life span, for example, child welfare services, services for youth, adult and family services, and services for the aged. The special tasks and circumstances associated with these age statuses has led to an emerging literature on gay and bisexual issues across the life span (Herdt & Boxer, 1992). Although research on the life span tends to stress problems, there is no reason why a life span orientation could not also focus on strengths and resources in individuals and/or their environments.

An emphasis on the life span raises strategic issues in doing research. While there is enormous practical importance for studying child and adolescent sexuality, for instance, the barriers to it are steep indeed. We will take the easy way out by not addressing these strategic dilemmas. We will limit ourselves to identifying themes in need of study in the hope that the obstacles to research will continue to fall as the lesbian and gay movement continues its push forward.

Childhood

Although the origins of homosexuality are not clear, gender non-conformity in childhood appears to be a significant, though not necessary, predictor of adult homosexual conduct (Friedman, 1988). Although most of the evidence for this is self-reported, retrospection by adult gay men, longitudinal studies of "sissy boys," extreme cases of gender non-conformity, corroborate the hypothesis. Upwards of 70% of sissy boys turn out to be gay or bisexual in adulthood (Money & Russo, 1979; Zuger, 1984; Green, 1985).

Gender non-conforming children are likely to find their way into services as "non-traditional boys" (Coleman, 1986). They pose difficult problems for the practitioner in that the desire for gender-conformity by parents may be contradicted by a lack of concern on the part of the child. Furthermore, given that childhood gender non-conformity is a far from perfect predictor of adult homosexuality, practitioners must be careful not to prematurely label a child while holding open the promise that good mental health does not depend on sexual orientation.

For our purposes, we do not know whether gender non-conformity in childhood varies across race and ethnicity. Films like *Paris Is Burning* give the impression that gender non-conformity is higher among African and Puerto Rican American youth, yet generalizations based on ethnographic data such as these are very unreliable. Without systematic cross-group and cross-class comparisons the question cannot be addressed. Similarly, the study of gender non-conformity in children should not be studied outside the context of family. Research on possible cultural variations in the way gender non-conformity is understood and dealt with in families is therefore of considerable importance.

Adolescence

Adolescence is a time when sexual desires and interests come to the fore. Cultural variation in age of initiation into sex suggests that African- and Latino-American boys will be involved in sex at an earlier age than white American boys (Hayes, 1987; Staples, 1982; Zelnik & Kanter, 1972). Little information is available on Native- and Asian-American boys. Cultural variations in age of initiation into sex can be studied as a way of understanding the risk associated with sexually transmitted diseases. Yet it might also serve other purposes. It can serve, for instance, for understanding the context of allegations of abuse and for understanding the context of normal sexual behavior in general.

The emotional turmoil associated with homosexual desires and initiation into homosexual sex is another important research area. Stage theorists often postulate that adolescents go through a period of confusion. In a homophobic society or sub-community that confusion may be heightened and lead to dire consequences. Researchers, for instance, find that homosexually inclined youth report high levels of suicidal ideation and gestures (Kournay, 1987). Because of this many believe that the increasingly high rates of suicide among youth are fueled by problems over sexual feelings (Rosenberh and Baer, 1989). Although the literature suggests that homosexual youth will have higher rates than heterosexual youth, studies in fact have yet to fully document this. Similarly, although Native American youth are believed to have higher rates of suicide and depression, cross-group comparisons have not actually been made. Studies of how gay adolescents of color react, and whether they are more or less likely to get depressed or contemplate suicide is therefore an important theme.

Suicide is not the only problem associated with initiation into homosexual conduct. The literature on runaway, street, and homeless youth, and teenage prostitution also point to issues of turmoil associated with initiation into sex. Although many families are supportive, many are not. There is evidence that the families of adolescents of color may be somewhat less likely to support a gay teenager than the families of white teenagers. This, however, has not been clearly documented.

Adults and Older Adults

As youth enter adulthood, issues related to coming out, partnering, and career become central. As adults pass into old age concerns turn to successful aging and death with dignity. Through adulthood the existence of strong support from friends and family assures healthy psychological development.

Coming Out. The study of the coming out process, including the extent to which gay men of color do come out, needs to be studied within the context of multiple identity formation. Models of identity formation, whether drawn up around the issue of gayness or around the issue of ethnicity, use a single dimensional representation of identity. Models of the coming out process can be criticized for their assumption that everyone who comes out is white American or that ethnicity is unrelated to coming out. Models of ethnic identity formation may also be criticized for their tendency to assume that all ethnic group members are heterosexual and that their identity is completely engulfed by considerations of ethnicity (E. Coleman, 1982; Phinney, 1990).

Partnering. The importance of intimate sexual relationships has been a central issue in human development. Erikson (1968) identified the search for intimacy and the avoidance of isolation as the central crisis of young adulthood. Given the changes in sexual mores that have taken place over the past few decades, the search for intimacy is now an important theme throughout adulthood. The way ethnic stratification and cultural mores shape this experience needs to be understood. Research attention should be given to understanding how important intimate relations are to gay men of color, how they go about meeting other men, how they settle with particular men, and how long-term those relationships are. Similarly, we need to focus on how traditions within ethnic communities and within the gay community facilitate the formation of long-term relationships among gay men.

Work and Career. Given that many if not most gay men do not raise children, their generative needs will likely be met through their occupations. Although there is considerable speculation about the occupations, incomes and wealth of gay men, studies have tended to report measures of central tendency (means and medians). Studies on the differences among gay men also must be done to determine the extent to which economic resources are distributed. Along these lines we need to document educational levels, employment and unemployment patterns, as well as satisfaction with employment and opportunities for advancement.

Retirement and Old Age. It is now clear that psychological development can continue even as the ravages of age force us into physical decline. Successful aging, that is, continuing to live productive and meaningful lives, is the desired outcome for services to the elderly. Successful aging is itself a function of having cherished intimate relations, accumulating material resources through a successful career, and having had the leisure time necessary to maintain oneself in a fit physical condition. In a society that often discriminates on the basis of age, obstacles to successful aging come in many forms: intimates and friends may die, material resources may either be absent or dwindle, the services necessary to maintain a healthy body may be inadequate. Worse, elderly people may become victims as others, often family members, neglect them or take advantage of them physically, psychologically, or financially. Isolated and frail elderly may become victims of their own failing abilities as, unable to care for themselves and having no one to care for them, they become the self-neglected so common in services for the elderly.

What little we know about aging among gays and lesbians and among people of color suggests that they lead productive and meaningful lives (Berger, 1984). Gay men of color have not been studied and so research into the way they age, the problems they confront and the strengths they draw on is necessary.

SOCIAL SERVICE DELIVERY ISSUES

Research shows that although need is the principal determinant of service use, psychological and social enabling factors are also important. Beyond identifying needs and strengths, therefore, a research agenda for the social services must incorporate studies on those factors that facilitate service use. Two important research areas follow from this: research on the ways men of color seek and accept help and research on the ways formal services are offered and delivered.

Help Seeking and Accepting Behavior

Problems are experienced as personal and social events. They are personal, because problems create discomfort and pain and provoke the need for amelioration. They are social in that the meaning attributed to problems and the attitudes associated with problem-solving often require confirmation from significant others. We know, for instance, that culture–mediated by interpersonal relations–influences the way people define their experiences, convert experiences into problems, and think about ways to solve the experiences considered problems (J. W. Green, 1982).

The literature on help seeking incorporates three important areas that we believe should be studied with regard to gay men of color. First, we need to understand how culture and social status influence the way individual experiences become identified as problems. American social services operate on a set of assumptions about the nature of problems that may or may not hold true for homosexually active men of color. Such assumptions may range from the meaning of mental illness and mental disorders, to the meaning of alcohol use and abuse, to the desire for individual autonomy and self-actualization. Within the sphere of homosexuality, such assumptions may range from attitudes about dress and comportment, to attitudes about the importance of gay friendships and relationships, to attitudes about coming out, or attitudes about appropriate behaviors in the sex act. Although we have recognized that the gay rights movement is having an international impact, we should not assume that all gay men understand problem behaviors in the same way.

Second, given that an experience is interpreted as a problem, the attitudes men may have about seeking help can vary in complex ways. For many immigrants and refugees the idea of going to a formal social service is beyond the realm of possibility. Even for men born in the United States, community attitudes about individual responsibility, the use of family and friends, or the use of indigenous forms of helper such as curanderos, root workers or shamans may preclude the possibility of turning to people in the university-credentialed helping professions. The fact that we are focusing on homosexually active men may complicate considerations about help seeking and accepting. Some men may be so tied to their ethnic communities that they would never consider using services provided through the gay and lesbian community. Other men, however, may feel that the stigma attached to homosexual conduct in their ethnic communities prevents them from using social services organized through those communities.

Third, the way men define a satisfactory way of giving help and a satisfactory resolution to a problem is also an important area of research. We cannot be sure that many of the common procedures used in the social services have equal appeal to men of color. Talk therapies and reflective sharing experiences, the use of first names and informality, being indirect and encouraging self-determination through group processes, may not be considered appropriate or useful by men of color. The most common procedures used in the social services may not have appeal for men of color.

Help Giving

The flip side of help seeking and accepting is help giving and service processing. Where help seeking research focuses on the psychosocial characteristics of clients and their communities, help giving research focuses on the characteristics of agencies and the services they provide. If the social services are to help men of color, they must have in place policies and procedures that will encourage men to use the service and once using, to successfully complete the service.

The range of research issues relating to service giving and processing are vast. They can range from the geography of giving, to the economics, technology, sociology, and politics of giving. Where services are located and the costs of services are of obvious consideration. The technology of giving–the actual nature of the services provided from outreach, to intake, through the particular types of services or interventions offered need to be studied to assess their cultural appropriateness and determine equity in service provision.

The sociology of giving includes the study of the attitudes and competencies of those who provide services. A number of studies have suggested that service personnel operate from stereotypes and in other ways misdiagnose or mistreat people of color (Bell & Mehta, 1981; Close, 1983; Hogan & Siu, 1988).

EFFECTIVE SERVICE OUTCOMES

The crucial element in service delivery is service effectiveness. The social services are constantly under pressure to prove their effectiveness. Although there is ample evidence that clients report satisfaction with the services they receive, and that service processing meets the demands of a public in need of service, there is little evidence that the lives of clients are improved as a result of their experiences in services. Certainly, it is not clear that social services have been able to significantly reduce such gnawing social problems as poverty, crime and drug use or increase the likelihood that families and couples will function better. At best the social services act as a band-aid, helping a myriad of people solve immediate crises, but not making much of a dent in preventing problems. In truth, social service technology cannot be expected to overcome what may in the end be political and economic problems; problems in a class-dominated, racist, sexist, and homophobic free market economy. Yet evaluation studies are needed if for no other reason than that they force us to confront the limitations of the social services.

METHODOLOGICAL ISSUES

It is common to hear that traditional research methodologies are inherently biased against people of color. Those who believe this generally assert that more non-positivist and qualitative research strategies need to be promoted. In a recent debate, however, Ashford (1994) and Sohng (1994) agreed that all forms of research methods were relevant. Ashford, arguing in support of traditional methodologies, asserts "that there is not a distinct methodology of science for studying the concerns of minorities and women" (p. 29).

Sohng, in spite of arguing that traditional research methods are inherently biased, nevertheless states that a unique minority perspective "does not specify particular research designs, measures, or data analysis techniques" (p. 28).

We also believe that the problem of researcher bias has to do more with the political economy of science rather than the methodology used. Qualitative and quantitative research can both be faulted. It is not the methods themselves so much as the sensitivity with which methods are used that creates bias. Following Sohng (1994), research on men of color should aspire to three objectives. First, the behavior of men of color should be studied within the context of the ethnic and racial stratification system which dominates American society. Men of color generally live out their lives with relatively less power and relatively less educational and occupational opportunities than white men and this needs to be taken into consideration. Second, research on men of color should foster cultural pluralism. The purpose of research should not be to encourage assimilation into mainstream norms but to allow for individual and collective self-determination. The purpose of research on gay men of color should not be to assure that they become attached to the gay community or that they become gay identified. Gay men of color, as they are doing, should be encouraged to seek their own individual and collective solutions to the problems they experience. Third, research on men of color should be carried out in an ethical way. Human subject reviews help to assure that no unfair advantage is taken of research subjects. On the other hand, there are more subtle forms of unethical behavior that researchers have to be wary of. Paramount among these may be the relative power and control of researchers and subjects. It is important, for instance, that advisory boards be set up to assure community input into the issues to be studied, the procedures used in the study, and the dissemination of study results.

Improving the Quality of Research

Although the amount of research on gay men has increased over the past decades, the quality of that research may not have progressed a great deal. This is especially the case with sampling procedures. The Achilles' heel of research on gay men has been the inability to use random sampling techniques. The result of this is that most studies reflect the behaviors, values and needs of white, middle class men. Similarly, since research on gay men tends to be non-comparative, research has tended to focus on a narrow range of gay-specific subjects.

Two recent advances suggest that these weaknesses can be overcome. Marketing researchers and political analysts (Elliott, 1994), who have long used random sampling techniques, have successfully begun to mainstream questions on sexual orientation much as they already do with race, gender, age, and occupation. As random sampling procedures have long used over-sampling techniques to increase the number of racial and ethnic minorities in a sample, these procedures can be used to assure that gay men of color are adequately sampled. The effect of these advances is that we are developing better data on a wider range of subjects.

These advances should be encouraged not only for large survey studies but for smaller experimental and non-experimental studies. Ethnographic and other qualitative researchers, for instance, must also be sensitive to sampling procedures so that they can address the generalizability of their findings.

On the other hand, there are trade-offs that need to be acknowledged such that we should not see mainstreaming and random sampling as a panacea. For instance, random sampling is effective to the extent that ethnic and racial minorities live in identifiable segregated areas. Men of color who do not live in segregated enclaves may become harder to locate through random techniques. Secondly, mainstreaming leads to studies where minorities are always compared to majorities. Comparative studies are extremely important not only because they allow us to understand cross-group differences but they make policy formulation and program planning easier. Nevertheless, there will continue to be need for non-comparative studies where specific groups of gay men of color are studied on their own terms. In this way their own special issues will more readily surface.

CONCLUSIONS AND RECOMMENDATIONS

There is a vast historical and anthropological literature that suggests that homosexual conduct is a universal phenomenon. Certainly, it is universal among the groups that have immigrated or been incorporated into the United States. Nevertheless, cultural norms around the expression of homosexuality and especially around the idea of a homosexual identity may be expected to vary. The degree to which American men vary, however, is unknown owing to the influence of the Gay and Lesbian Movement. Men of color whose origin in the United States goes back one or more generations are likely to be strongly influenced by the mores being developed in the gay and lesbian communities. New immigrants are also likely to have been influenced by European and American ideas and may even have immigrated because of these influences. Services should probably assume that at least some men of color will rely heavily on their ethnic traditions in understanding homosexual conduct. Most men of color, however, are likely to fall somewhere in between, neither entirely traditional nor entirely "Americanized" in their ideas. A central focus of research, therefore, is to clarify the range of meanings men of color apply to homosexual conduct and identity.

A problem-solving model may be fruitfully used to set an applied research agenda. Using this framework, we have identified a wide range of research themes. With regard to the study of problems and strengths we suggest studies on health and mental health problems, studies on basic and higher order needs, and studies on issues across the life span. With regard to service planning and intervention, we suggest that the issues of help seeking, help giving, and help accepting be studied. The need for good outcome evaluation studies cannot be overlooked.

Although we have identified an ambitious set of topics, we do not prioritize these. Most of the recent research has focused on AIDS prevention and amelioration and this is understandable given the significance of this disease. We suspect that immediate needs will always drive the research agenda. On the other hand, researchers should continue to chip away at all the topics outlined here so that we can continually grow in our knowledge of research.

There is no one type of research that is appropriate to gay men of color. Researchers, however, must be sensitive that part of their duty is to help assure that men of color will be understood within the context of their minority status and provided with opportunities to participate fully in American life.

REFERENCES

Ashford, J. B. (1994). Are traditional empirical research methods inherently biased against people of color? "No," in W. W. Hudson & P. S. Nurius (Eds.), *Controversial issues in social work research* (pp. 27-33). Boston, MA: Allyn & Bacon.

Bell, C. C., & Mehta, H. (1981). The misdiagnosis of black patients with manic depressive symptoms. *Journal of the National Medical Association, 72*(2), 1980.

Bell, A. P., & Weinberg, M. S. (1978). *Homosexualities.* New York: Simon & Schuster.

Berger, R. M. (1984). Realities of gay and lesbian aging. *Social Work, 29*(1), 57-62.

Billy, J. O. G., Tanfer, K., Grady, W. R., & Klepinger, D. H. (1993). The sexual behavior of men in the United States. *Family Planning Perspectives, 25*(2), 52-60.

Centers for Disease Control and Prevention. (1994). AIDS among racial/ethnic minorities–United States, 1993. *Morbidity and Mortality Weekly Report, 43*(35), 644-647, 653-655.

Chu, S. Y., Peterman, T. A., Doll, L. S., Buehler, J. W., & Curran, J. W. (1992). AIDS in bisexual men in the United States: Epidemiology and transmission to women. *American Journal of Public Health, 82*(2), 220-224.

Close, M. M. (1983). Child welfare and people of color: Denial of equal access. *Social Work Research and Abstracts, 19*(4), 13-20.

Coleman, E. (1982). Developmental stages of the coming-out process. *American Behavioral Scientist, 25*(4), 469-82.

Coleman, M. (1986). Nontraditional boys: A minority in need of reassessment. *Child Welfare, 65*(3), 252-258.

Duberman, M., Vicinus, M. & Chauncey, C., Jr. (1989). *Hidden from history: Reclaiming the gay & lesbian past.* New York: Meridian.

Dynes, W. R. (1987). *Homosexuality: A research guide.* New York: Garland Publishing.

Elliott, S. (1994, June 9). A sharper view of gay consumers. *New York Times*, pp. C1-4.

Erikson, E. H. (1968). Life cycle. In D. L. Sills (Ed.). *The International Encyclopedia of the Social Sciences* (pp. 286-292). New York: Macmillan.

Friedman, R. C. (1988). *Male Homosexuality: A contemporary psychoanalytic perspective.* New Haven: Yale University Press.

Gebhard, P. H., & Johnson, A. B. (1979). *The Kinsey data: Marginal tabulations of the 1938-1963 interviews conducted by the Institute for Sex Research.* Philadelphia: Saunders.

Green, J. W. (1982). Help seeking behavior. In J. W. Green (Ed.), *Cultural awareness in the social services* (pp. 32-48). Englewood Cliffs, NJ: Prentice Hall.

Green, R. (1985). *The "sissy boy syndrome" and the development of homosexuality.* New Haven: Yale University Press.

Greenberg, D. F. (1988). *The construction of homosexuality.* Chicago: University of Chicago Press.

Harry, J. (1990). A probability sample of gay males. *Journal of Homosexuality, 19*(1), 89-104.

Hartman, A., & Laird, J. (1983). *Family centered social work practice.* New York: Free Press.

Haynes, K. C. (1988). Minorities, intravenous drug users, and AIDS: A review. *Multicultural Inquiry and Research on AIDS, 2*(4), 1-2.

Herdt, G., & Boxer, A. (1992). Culture, history, and life course of gay men. In G. Herdt (Ed.), *Gay culture in America: Essays from the field* (pp. 1-28). Boston: Beacon.

Hogan, P. T., & Siu, S. (1988). Minority children and the welfare system: An historical perspective. *Social Work, 33*(6), 493-498.

Johnson, J. (1982). Influence of assimilation on the psychosocial adjustment of black homosexual men. *Dissertation Abstracts International, 42,* 4620B.

Karon, J. M., & Berkelman, R. L. (1991). The geographic and ethnic diversity of AIDS incidence trends in homosexual/bisexual men in the United States. *Journal of Acquired Immune Deficiency Syndromes, 4*(12), 1179-1189.

Katz, J. (1976). *Gay American history: Lesbians and gay men in the U.S.A.* New York: Avon.

Kinsey, A. C., Pomeroy, W. B., & Martin, C. E. (1948). *Sexual behavior in the human male.* Philadelphia: W. B. Saunders.

Kournay, R. F. C. (1989). Suicide among homosexual adolescents. *Journal of Homosexuality, 13*(4), 111-117.

Luczak, R. (Ed.). (1993). *Eyes of desire.* Boston: Alyson.

Maslow, A. H. (1954). *Motivation and personality.* New York: Harper & Row.

Mead, M. (1935). *Sex and temperament.* New York: Morrow.

Money, J., & Russo, A. J. (1979). Homosexual outcome of discordant gender activity role in childhood: Longitudinal follow-up. *Journal of Pediatric Psychology, 4,* 29-49.

Phinney, J. S. (1990). Ethnic identity in adolescents and adults: Review of research. *Psychological Bulletin, 108,* (3).

Rosenberg, M. L., & Baer, K. (Eds.). *Report of the Secretary's Task Force on Youth Suicide, Vol 3.* (DHHS Publications No. ADM 89-1621). Washington, DC: Superintendent of Documents.

Sohng, S. (1994). Are traditional empirical research methods inherently biased against people of color? "Yes," In W. W. Hudson & P. S. Nurius (Eds.), *Controversial issues in social work research* (pp. 22-27). Boston: Allyn & Bacon.

Staples, R. (1982). *Black masculinity: The black male's role in American society.* San Francisco: The Black Scholar Press.

Williams, W. L. (1986). *The spirit and the flesh: Sexual diversity in American Indian culture.* Boston, MA: Beacon Press.

Zelnik, M., & Kanter, J. (1972). *Sexuality, contraception, and pregnancy among young unwed females in the United States.* Unpublished manuscript.

Zuger, B. (1984). Early effeminate behavior in boys: Outcomes and significance for homosexuality. *Journal of Nervous Mental Disorders, 172*(2), 90-97.

Index

Notes: Page numbers followed by "n" indicate footnoted information.

Page numbers preceded by *mentioned* indicate intermittent discussion of the subject on each of the inclusive pages.

Personal names cited in full, and titles of published and media works cited in the text, are indexed; however, surname-only and reference source-related citations are not indexed.

Haworth
DOCUMENT DELIVERY
SERVICE

This valuable service provides a single-article order form for any article from a Haworth journal.

- *Time Saving:* No running around from library to library to find a specific article.
- *Cost Effective:* All costs are kept down to a minimum.
- *Fast Delivery:* Choose from several options, including same-day FAX.
- *No Copyright Hassles:* You will be supplied by the original publisher.
- *Easy Payment:* Choose from several easy payment methods.

Open Accounts Welcome for ...
- Library Interlibrary Loan Departments
- Library Network/Consortia Wishing to Provide Single-Article Services
- Indexing/Abstracting Services with Single Article Provision Services
- Document Provision Brokers and Freelance Information Service Providers

---

MAIL or *FAX* THIS ENTIRE ORDER FORM TO:

Haworth Document Delivery Service
The Haworth Press, Inc.
10 Alice Street
Binghamton, NY 13904-1580

or FAX: 1-800-895-0582
or CALL: 1-800-342-9678
9am-5pm EST

PLEASE SEND ME PHOTOCOPIES OF THE FOLLOWING SINGLE ARTICLES:

1) Journal Title: _____
   Vol/Issue/Year:_____ Starting & Ending Pages:_____
   Article Title:_____

2) Journal Title: _____
   Vol/Issue/Year:_____ Starting & Ending Pages:_____
   Article Title:_____

3) Journal Title: _____
   Vol/Issue/Year:_____ Starting & Ending Pages:_____
   Article Title:_____

4) Journal Title: _____
   Vol/Issue/Year:_____ Starting & Ending Pages:_____
   Article Title:_____

(See other side for Costs and Payment Information)

COSTS: Please figure your cost to order quality copies of an article.

1. Set-up charge per article: $8.00
   ($8.00 × number of separate articles)   _____

2. Photocopying charge for each article:
   1-10 pages: $1.00   _____

   11-19 pages: $3.00   _____

   20-29 pages: $5.00   _____

   30+ pages: $2.00/10 pages   _____

3. Flexicover (optional): $2.00/article   _____

4. Postage & Handling: US: $1.00 for the first article/
                       $.50 each additional article _____

   Federal Express: $25.00   _____

   Outside US: $2.00 for first article/
               $.50 each additional article _____

5. Same-day FAX service: $.35 per page   _____

                    GRAND TOTAL: _____

METHOD OF PAYMENT: (please check one)

❑ Check enclosed   ❑ Please ship and bill. PO # _____
                    (sorry we can ship and bill to bookstores only! All others must pre-pay)

❑ Charge to my credit card: ❑ Visa;   ❑ MasterCard;   ❑ Discover;
                             ❑ American Express;

Account Number: _____ Expiration date: _____

Signature: X_____

Name: _____ Institution: _____

Address: _____

_____

City: _____ State: _____ Zip: _____

Phone Number: _____ FAX Number: _____

MAIL or *FAX* THIS ENTIRE ORDER FORM TO:

Haworth Document Delivery Service	**or FAX:** 1-800-895-0582
The Haworth Press, Inc.	**or CALL:** 1-800-342-9678
10 Alice Street	9am-5pm EST)
Binghamton, NY 13904-1580	